The Gentle Art of Stitching

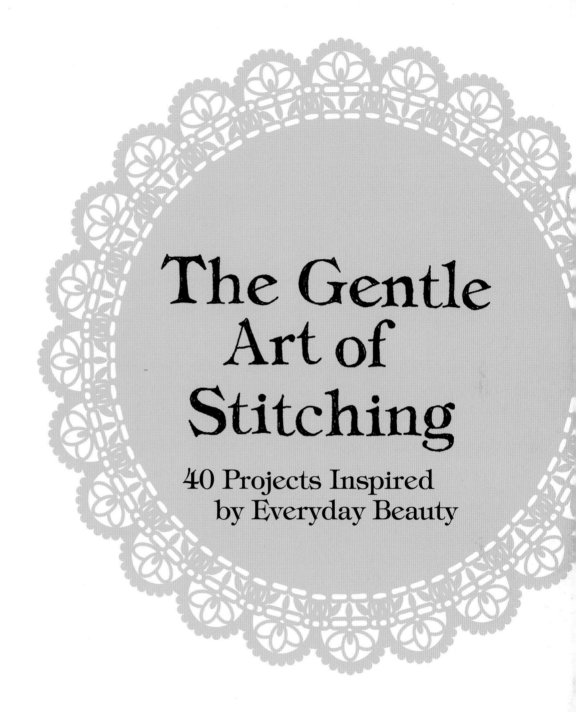

The Gentle Art of Stitching

40 Projects Inspired by Everyday Beauty

Jane Brocket

COLLINS & BROWN

Contents

Introduction

Stitching is the gentlest of the 'gentle arts'. The term 'gentle arts' was used in the nineteenth century to describe stitching and other creative decorative 'work' such as crochet, lace-making and knitting done by ladies and young girls. I have adopted it here to suggest not only the continuity with, and links to, earlier needlewomen, but also to convey the idea of stitching as a quietly enjoyable, non-competitive, unstressed and relaxing pastime.

Gentle stitching is not fraught, demanding or nerve-jangling. Instead it is simple, straightforward — something that can be done while relaxing, talking, sitting in the sunshine or on holiday. It doesn't require great amounts of skill, confidence or planning and is best started by simply threading a needle, abandoning high expectations and creating stitches on a nice piece of fabric. Gentle stitching is easy-going and anxiety-free, and focuses on the very essence of stitching without extra processes, equipment and complex patterns. It aims not to ruin your eyesight or to create tension, but to offer scope for self-expression, and an opportunity to make and embellish in a gently old-fashioned way.

My aim in this book is to celebrate the beauty, variety and versatility of the stitch itself, in the context of simple, manageable projects. After many years with needle and thread and having been put off too often by the so-called 'correct' ways of doing things, I realised that the real delight of gentle stitching by hand is nothing to do with degree of difficulty or with virtuoso needlework, but in watching the stitches form right before your eyes, in getting close to and enjoying every one as you work. Stitching by its very nature is often on a small scale; it can take a while to cover surfaces and reach the end. So, rather than wish it were otherwise, I find it's better to take pleasure in the processes and rhythms, to focus on the meditative, repetitive nature of gentle stitching and to enliven it with beautiful colours, a mix of stitches and, on occasion, the thrill of making it up as you go along. It doesn't have to be small-scale, either, as it's possible to apply big, bold stitches over larger surfaces and cover them relatively quickly, and I include inspiration and directions for projects that are easily completed. Even the most time-consuming design in the book, a needlepoint cushion cover, can be completed in four weeks, which is a lot less time than most needlepoint cushions (more like four years). (I have also given instructions on how to finish it at home, thus avoiding the fate of most needlepoint pieces, which languish, unstretched and unmade-up, in a bag in a cupboard.)

My own stitching history began when I was five. Encouraged and guided by my nana, Alice Twist, I made little felt needlebooks to sell for sixpence to relatives, including my very patient and obliging nana, whose materials I used. At junior school, I progressed to binka canvas samplers and loved the freedom of creating my own stitches on the structured canvas background, although I would have given a great deal to add more colours beyond the school-issue red, green and blue. I then went from this can-do, creative, colourful exploration of stitching to the type of senior school needlework lessons that dent the confidence of young stitchers and turn needlework into a battleground of rules and correctness. It took me years to regain my confidence, and to see that having a good time with a needle and thread was just as valuable a way of stitching as creating skilful, accurate work.

There was then a gap in my stitching career until I had to go into hospital in my late twenties. I took some cross stitch with me and although this remains unfinished to this day, it reignited my interest in stitching. This was further fuelled by a short period working for Arthur Sanderson & Sons, who owned the William Morris design archives. I was fascinated by his embroidery designs and the stitching of his wife, Jane, and daughter, May. Reading about the exquisite work of these exceptionally talented needlewomen led me to the late nineteenth-century Scottish 'art' embroiderers such as Jessie Newberry, Anne Macbeth, Phoebe Anna Traquair and Margaret MacDonald (wife of Charles Rennie Mackintosh).

I admired their skill and their concentration on beautiful, classic stitches and simple designs, and was inspired by them to acquire some decent stitching skills. After living abroad for six years we moved back to England, not too far from the

Royal School of Needlework at Hampton Court Palace, and I decided to re-start my stitching with traditional pictorial embroidery. I have always liked vintage cottage garden embroideries and began stitching little herbaceous borders and vegetable plots that practised the stitches I was teaching myself from books. I also had a few lessons at the highly prestigious RSN; I learned a great deal, but after one particular two-day course in which I barely finished a single pansy, I decided the immaculate approach was not for me.

Fortunately, I soon discovered that there were courses and workshops for more relaxed, easy-going stitchers who were interested in exploring the possibility of creating stitched textiles using colour, interesting fabrics and simple ideas. West Dean College in Sussex had, and still has, a fantastic programme of stitching weekends, and I attended some of these. I even went as far as a preparatory course for a City and Guilds qualification, but after several weeks of burning fabric and not even threading a needle, I gave up and went back to my cottage gardens.

When I started making quilts about eight years ago, I discovered the delights of hand-stitching on a large scale. Although I machine-piece the tops, I don't machine-quilt because I really enjoy the sheer freedom of making lines of running stitch up and down and across lovely fabrics. Coming back to the humble running stitch reminded me of the real pleasures of this type of gentle stitching: the handling of fabrics, the choosing of threads, the joy of colour, the close work and the textured and very unapologetically visible results.

Now, having hand-quilted goodness knows how many quilts and attended a fair few ultra-relaxed, highly inspirational stitching weekends and workshops with marvellous teachers such as Janet Bolton and Julie Arkell, I have come to realise what the formula for gentle stitching should include. And it is this: simplicity, colour, good threads, some stitch variety but nothing too complex, getting started without too much of a plan (and not being held back by too much of a plan), hand-drawn designs, old-fashioned alphabets, practical and available fabrics, useful projects. It should avoid: time-consuming setting up and finishing, complicated charts, very fine threads and fabrics, projects for items that will gather dust, anything that induces fear and anxiety.

So in this book there is no emphasis on a single type of stitching, but rather a range of different techniques and traditions, all of which are suitable for a beginner as well as for someone who already enjoys stitching and wants to be more freewheeling and self-directed. The projects encourage the reader to have a go, to work with the skills you already have, no matter how unrefined or unpractised. They focus on the delight of wielding a needle and thread to make, decorate, embellish, enhance and recycle. Most of the projects can be done entirely by hand, and none require complicated stitches or techniques. In fact, if all you can do or like to do is running stitch, you will find plenty of ideas. And if you like more adventurous French knots and cross stitch, there are projects for you, too.

Above all, my aim has been to keep to easy but effective hand-stitching, to concentrate on doable, colourful, straightforward projects that can be made with easy-to-obtain materials and equipment, and I have dispensed with many rules, methods and charts. There is no need for any professional finishing with any of the projects, nor is there any call for special materials other than lovely fabrics and threads, and the occasional hoop and task-specific needle (all the materials are widely available in shops or on the internet). And I hope that when you have found your stitching rhythm and style, the projects shown here will inspire you to branch out and stitch your own ideas. Because that's what it's all about: happy, gentle stitching.

So choose your fabric and a stitch, thread a needle and get going.

Jane Brocket
Spring 2012

The sewing box

Do people still have dedicated sewing boxes? Perhaps 1960s-style wooden ones with spindly legs and tops that roll back to reveal little compartments full of assorted haberdashery? Or the painted, woven wicker type with padded pink or peach satin lids full of pins and needles trailing little lengths of thread, and a removable tray which reveals, like a two-tier chocolate box, another layer of goodies underneath? Or battered but treasured biscuit tins, saved from a Christmas many years ago, filled with a glorious pick 'n' mix selection of buttons and bobbins and bits and pieces? To answer my own question, I think many sewers must have one, because a sewing box is also a box of treasure, and which stitcher wouldn't want one of those?

I have many happy memories of sorting out my mum's sewing box (very much the wicker basket variety but lined with bright yellow satin). I recall being asked every so often to tidy it and not wanting to do so, but each time I soon became engrossed in unravelling, winding, sorting out, matching and arranging. It was a matter of great pride to have it looking immaculate when I'd finished. I think this is where my interest in haberdashery comes from: handling and scrutinising all those Sylko threads, different packs of needles, assorted buttons and fabric tape measures (always stopping to measure various part of myself) made me realise how nice it is to have everything you need for sewing and stitching in one place.

These days, though, my sewing bits and bobs are kept in different places because I hate to imagine the chaos that would develop inside a single container. My sewing box is an old wooden writing box, with internal compartments and drawers and secret sections that hold general cottons and children's name tapes. I keep my embroidery threads in a metal office cabinet that has fifteen little drawers (with drawers for tiny beads, larger beads, vintage transfers, silk threads, buttons to be covered). In another cabinet (a wonderful set of vintage, glass-fronted drapers' drawers that is one of the best investments I ever made), I have a drawer for buttons, one for machine-embroidery threads, one for tapestry threads and one for ribbons. I keep scissors in old golden syrup tins because if I don't keep an eye on them, they disappear. And as I hate fiddling about looking for sharp objects at the bottom of a box or tin, I keep all my pins in pincushions or stuck in the padded armrest of whichever settee I happen to be sitting on, something I think is very practical but which does seem to shock some people.

But the principle of a sewing box remains essential as a way of organising your stitching supplies, no matter what sort of receptacle or however many receptacles you choose to have. Thankfully, one of the great things about stitching is that you really don't need much to get started. A needle and thread, some fabric and a pair of sharp scissors are all that's required. Of course, there are always many more things you can buy as you go along, but I prefer to concentrate on lovely threads and fabrics rather than expensive frames and fiddly needle threaders that don't work. The following is a list of indispensable items, plus a few luxuries.

The ideal sewing box/ basket/drawer

Whatever you use is a matter of personal preference or what you can find. Vintage sewing boxes and baskets can be bought cheaply, and it's always nice to reuse something such as a set of old biscuit tins for buttons and threads and needles. Food tins such as golden syrup tins make excellent containers, and little bowls from the kitchen are ideal for keeping needles in while you sew a project.

Needles

I have never fully subscribed to the idea that there is a 'correct' needle for every type of stitching. This is probably because I have never quite understood the minute differences between all the various needles on sale in a good haberdashery department or shop. My rule of thumb for all general stitching is to use what feels best for the job and to be guided by what works most comfortably. For example, I find working with very short quilting needles very uncomfortable so I hand-quilt with whichever longer 'sharp' or general-purpose needle works well, generally the thinner the better. In fact, nearly all my needles are basic sharps, embroidery and crewel needles bought in packs of mixed sizes so that I can pick what suits the job in hand (and because I have never committed to memory which number goes with which sort of fabric). The size to use depends on the quality of your eyesight, the thickness of the thread and the fineness of the fabric. It's important to be able to thread the needle relatively easily, and a needle should never leave a hole in the fabric. If either or both of these problems are happening, it's best to change the needle. Brand-wise it does pay to buy good-quality needles from

reputable makers; I particularly like John James and Clover. As needles are so important to happy stitching and are very cheap, it is worth paying a few pence extra for good needles.

However, there are a few exceptions to the above that are worth mentioning:

❖ Needlepoint and canvas work (such as binka stitching, see page 90) require needles sold as tapestry needles, which have large eyes and blunt points. The thicker the thread, the chunkier the needle needs to be.

❖ Cross stitch needles make a huge difference to the pleasure and ease of cross stitching (see page 127). They are very fine but have slightly rounded tips so the needle is much easier to place in the relevant hole or space and there is less likelihood of it splitting a stitch or canvas thread. John James makes fantastic cross stitch needles and I find a 24 or a 26 works well with cotton perlé 8 or three strands of embroidery thread on 14-count Aida or 28-count Dublin evenweave linen.

❖ Finally, sashiko needles are undoubtedly the best to use for sashiko stitching as they are super-sharp and strong and enable you to 'load' the needle before pulling it through (see page 22), so are definitely worth seeking out (Olympus and Clover both make excellent, shockingly sharp sashiko needles).

Threads

Again, it's quite possible to create all sorts of effects with different types of stitching using just a few mainstay threads. Much as I like experimenting, I have discovered that the affordable, widely available basics are the best; lovely, rare threads may be very tempting but when you add up how much it will cost to stitch a project of any decent size, they can be prohibitively expensive.

All the projects in this book can be stitched with substitute threads. Please do not feel you must use what I have used. Plus, it's always exciting to see what is available where you are and to use equivalents.

These are the threads in my sewing box.

❖ Basic 100 per cent all-purpose sewing thread for machine-sewing. I prefer Gütterman, although I see that several big brands are going back to 100 per cent cotton after years in a polyester wilderness.

❖ 100 per cent cotton quilting thread. Again, I like Gütterman, but I prefer the very smooth Mettler threads if I can find them. Quilting thread is stronger than standard everyday cotton thread, and it is also useful when you are mounting pieces of work on to thick cardboard as quilting thread can be pulled hard without fear of it snapping.

❖ Stranded cotton (often known as embroidery cotton, embroidery silk or embroidery floss). This is made up of six strands that can be separated and is the basis of much domestic embroidery. Two major brands, DMC and Anchor, are widely available. Although it's possible to find cheaper stranded cotton, the big brands are worth buying because they are high quality and colourfast, plus they come in hundreds of fabulous colours. (Note that the reference numbers for each colour are not the same for the two brands.)

The only problem with stranded cottons is that the skeins unwind very easily, the band with the reference numbers slides off, and the threads can all too easily end up in a huge tangle. The solution, if you are organised, is to buy packs of cardboard or thread tidies and wind embroidery thread on to them as soon as you have undone a skein (and write the name and number on the card). The cards are available from Amazon or haberdashery websites.

❖ Cotton perlé (also known as pearl cotton). Unlike stranded cotton, this cannot be separated, but instead is a twisted thread with a luminous sheen. It's a delight to stitch with and is ideal for all sorts of embroidery, cross stitch, hand-quilting, crazy quilting and chain stitch. It comes in lots of colours (but not as many as stranded cotton) and in a variety of thicknesses (3, 5, 8, 12, 16, with the lowest number being the thickest). I find 8 is a fantastic all-round thread and really enjoy using 5 when I want thickly defined stitching. DMC and Anchor produce good cotton perlé, but there are plenty of other good brands. I also recommend Finca cotton perlé for wonderful colours.

❖ Tapestry wools for needlepoint. Anchor and DMC are well-known brands and have a huge number of colours in their ranges. Appleton's tapestry wools are fabulous for quality and colour, but can be difficult to track down.

❖ Sashiko threads. Although generic soft, thick cotton threads can be used, I like the authentic sashiko threads from Japan (I buy the Olympus brand) because they are meant for the job, and I just can't resist the authentic packaging. Plus, Olympus make the very traditional off-white and indigo colours.

❖ Silk threads. I don't use a lot of silk thread because I find it can be very expensive. However, one of the biggest stitching treats I can think of is using silk threads on silk fabrics; they just glide through and make every stitch a real pleasure. Mulberry Silks sell silk thread in three thicknesses, and create the most wonderful subject and theme packs I have ever seen.

Pins

I gave up with standard-issue pins a long time ago and switched to the long, glass-headed variety not only for the pretty colours and visibility, but also for ease of handling. I use quilting pins nearly all the time except when they are too thick for a fine fabric, in which case I use fine quilting pins or silk pins, which are shorter. The Clover brand is particularly good for high-quality pins that are worth investing in, but any good haberdashery should have decent stainless-steel, glass-headed pins.

It goes without saying that it's best to keep pins in a pincushion or two as it's a horrible job trying to fish them out of the sides and bottom of a workbox or, worse still, from down the sides of chairs and settees.

Scissors

Many stitchers swear by their tiny, elaborately designed embroidery scissors, but I have always found them too small and dainty to use (they often need a 'scissor keeper' to prevent them getting lost but it beats me how anyone can use such minute scissors with a padded square hanging off them and getting in the way all the time). However, I have recently discovered that Prym make really good, plain and practical embroidery scissors which are very pointy, very sharp and very useful. Otherwise, I use basic, common-or-garden Fiskars scissors in various sizes. I put a short tag of wool on the newer ones so I can see immediately if they are being used for the wrong purposes.

A rotary cutter used with a quilter's ruler and a self-healing mat are fantastic for cutting fabrics, even if you are not making quilts.

Plus

❖ A long tape measure.
❖ Water-soluble, air-soluble or chalk pens for drawing designs on fabric. (See page 140 for more on using these.)

Nice haberdashery extras

It's all very well having the practical stuff in your sewing box, but what about the excitement of rummaging for buttons, beads, ribbons and all sorts of pretty extras? They are all part of the joy of stitching, and are what transforms a useful box into a box of treasure.

Whether or not you buy new or vintage or a mix is up to you. Old button cards, hooks and eyes, press-studs, woven name and initial tapes, vintage cards of darning thread, imperial tape measures, old wooden spools, and skeins and cards of linen thread all look amazing and are fast becoming collectors' items. But be wary of using old threads as they can often deteriorate over time and you may find they snap easily or break off mid-stitch. As for new goodies, there is always an excuse for a little paper bag of beautiful buttons, a metre or two of lovely ribbon, a pack of shimmering silk threads or a collection of gorgeously packaged Sajou threads.

Haberdashery

The gentle art of stitching is underpinned by haberdashery. Without easy access to needles and notions, buttons and bobbins, fabrics and fripperies, the stitcher is stuck. As well as being down-to-earth and useful, the haberdashery is a place of dreams where we can imagine and plan fabulous projects and devise clever ways of using the weird and wonderful things we find in there.

In my first book *The Gentle Art of Domesticity* (2007), I wrote a heartfelt defence of good, old-fashioned haberdashery shops and departments. The kind of place where you can take your time, where the tiniest purchase of a packet of needles, a skein of thread, a buckle or braid, is unhurried and of importance. Unfortunately, unless you live in a major city or a very unusual town, these days you are still unlikely to come across a marvellously old-fashioned, well-stocked haberdashery full of shoulder pads, studs, pipings, cords and suspender clips. Yet the popularity of vintage haberdashery and its modern-day equivalents has, if anything, grown in the intervening years since my book.

In this short time, there has been a pleasing growth in the demand for more than needles, pins and threads (which is pretty much what most haberdashery departments had dwindled to, if they hadn't been forced out of existence altogether), which has resulted in the emergence of some beautiful, modern, real and online haberdashery shops and departments, as well as the revitalisation of some well-established names.

The new haberdashers are likely to be young and energetic crafty people who not only appreciate the usefulness of their wares, but also love and value ribbons, bows and pretty extras. There is an art to stocking good haberdashery that involves knowing your customers and your customers' needs, uncovering new and vintage items and displaying them in the traditional, crammed sweet-shop style, and modern haberdasheries can be very seductive places. They don't have to be large or posh establishments, but the range should be thoughtfully chosen and clearly displayed.

There is nothing nicer than coming across little drawers of cotton perlé threads, racks of colourful skeins of embroidery floss, rotating stands of wools, tubes of buttons, jars of beads, little plastic containers of glass-headed pins and wheels of pearly pins, rolls of ribbons, cards of braids, little packets of needles, thimbles, super-sharp scissors and bolts of fabric — not to mention the inspiration they provide and their faith in the handmade — all gathered together in one magical place.

So if you come across one or are just lucky enough to have a local haberdashery, I say support it.

Home haberdashery

We all love a peek into someone else's creative space. That's why on blogs there is so much interest in the spaces where people make and stitch and paint, and why there is so much coverage in magazines of interesting studios, idiosyncratic rooms and corners. It is always fascinating to see how others organise their materials and supplies around them, so much so that there are several books devoted to the subject.

One American title that may induce some major space/fabric/haberdashery envy is *Where Women Create* by Jo Packham (Sterling, 2005), but it also presents all sorts of clever storage and presentation arrangements. These are the dream spaces, and more accessible to most is the way Julie Arkell arranges her supplies very simply on open shelves, in jam jars, newspaper-covered and papier mâché boxes (photos can be seen in her book *Julie Arkell — Home*, published by the Ruthin Craft Gallery). This simple, practical and economical system gives hope to everyone who may not have vast stocks or space or made-to-measure storage, and inspiration to create a home haberdashery of whatever scale is possible, whether it's a single shelf or a whole room.

It's often the little bits and pieces — buttons and ribbons and jars full of beads — that look lovely grouped together, so it's worth showing them off in arrangements of old boxes and tins and jam jars instead of hiding them away in drawers. Since the supplies themselves are the things of beauty, the containers don't have to be anything special; places like Ikea, homeware shops and stores, and even old-fashioned ironmongers selling drawers for screws and nails are great home haberdashery hunting grounds.

Old printer's trays, trays with compartments, thread cards, cards with buttons, biscuit tins, cake tins, wooden bobbin holders, home-made needle books and pincushions are all wonderful ways of displaying habby treasures.

Look out for and collect DIY hardware boxes with lots of compartments for nails and screws, jam jars, cardboard boxes with label slots, brown kraft paper boxes, cutlery trays (good for embroidery threads), wine and champagne gift boxes (for bobbins), golden syrup tins (crochet hooks, scissors), glass-top or clear-top tins in all sizes and shapes, chocolate boxes, shoeboxes and filing boxes.

Sashiko

The word 'sashiko' means 'stab stitch' or 'little stabs', which sums up the method of making lots of small, even stitches to build up distinctive and very traditional patterns, each of which has its own evocative name. How could 'Dragonfly Above the Earth', 'Blowing Grasses and Cherry Blossoms' or 'Seven Treasures of Buddha' not be inspirational?

For a while, I read a great deal about sashiko on craft blogs, but had never done any until recently. I knew it was a type of Japanese stitching that looked very beautiful and strikingly decorative but also, because of the way it was made up of lines of running stitch, that it was very appealingly simple. Nevertheless, as is so often the case when you want to try a new skill or craft, I didn't know where to begin. The prospect of having to substitute local materials for authentic Japanese supplies discouraged me, until I discovered that you can buy wonderful little Japanese sashiko kits and sashiko needles and thread quite easily outside Japan, and that these are all you need to get started.

Sashiko is an ancient form of stitching from Japan, a form of darning originally used by farmers and fishermen to reinforce and patch worn and damaged clothing. It is also used as a traditional type of quilting to create practical but decorative patterns, so could be said to be a combination of quilting, mending, beautifying and decorating. The distinctive look of sashiko comes from the consistency and very visibility of the stitching combined with the vast number of patterns — ancient and modern — to which it can be applied.

Stitching a sashiko kit

There are so many traditional sashiko patterns that the choice can be quite overwhelming for a beginner, and this is why a kit is a good way to start. The whole concept of using sashiko kits as samplers is widely accepted; the method of stitching on pre-printed fabric is not seen as a second-rate way of stitching, and the kits themselves come in an excellent range of designs. The most popular are sold under the Olympus brand, which produces all the classic, typically geometric and repeating sashiko patterns. The traditional patterns can also be bought as paper designs to be transferred to fabrics, and it's also possible to mark out large-scale versions with rulers and templates (both of these methods are much more time-consuming and require a good degree of patience and accuracy).

So when I wanted to get going with sashiko, I chose the easy kit route because the kits come with pre-printed, authentic Japanese sashiko fabric (see page 20). My favourite pattern is the 'Shippo Tsunagi' or 'Seven Treasures', which is made up of intersecting circles and is quite mesmerising to look at despite its simplicity.

It came as a 30cm (12in) square of soft, loosely woven indigo-blue cotton fabric, which is ideal for the thick and horribly sharp sashiko needles to get through, plus a skein of off-white cotton sashiko thread (I wanted to be as traditional as possible to begin with). I opened it up, threaded the needle and just started stitching along the lines.

I'd looked up a few basic directions beforehand, and was reassured by the fact that there is nothing too rule-like about sashiko (it's not imperative that you use any of the authentic Japanese materials, your stitch length/technique can suit your individual style and motion, a special thimble is optional). I soon discovered that sashiko is the most enjoyable sort of running stitch stitching I'd done since junior school. I quickly made up two kits (blue on white and white on blue) and then looked around for a different, more personal, but equally simple sashiko challenge.

Right: *Shippo Tsunagi* or 'Seven Treasures' sashiko kit.

To stitch non-kit sashiko

If you are beyond kits and/or want to make something larger using these or your own designs, here are the materials you will need.

Fabrics

If you can't find authentic Japanese sashiko fabric (which is available outside Japan and via websites, but not always easy to track down), you will need to choose a substitute. One of the advantages of starting with a kit is that it's possible to get a taste of working with the traditional fabric so you know what to look for, plus you can take the piece into fabric shops and find the closest match.

The ideal fabric is soft, medium-weight cotton with a relatively loose, open weave. It doesn't need to be anything spectacular or expensive as sashiko was never intended to be posh stitching, and in fact you are much more likely to find suitable fabrics in the lower price range. The needle must be able to go through the fabric with ease, always bearing in mind that the quite thick cotton sashiko thread is used double. The stitching should flow easily and if you find you have to pull and tug, the fabric is too fine. Cottons and linens or cotton/linen mixes (some good ones come from India) are the easiest to load on to the long needle and do not pucker up.

The choice of fabric colour is yours, but the traditional sashiko colours are indigo and ecru.

Left: *Shippo Tsunagi* or 'Seven Treasures' sashiko kit.

Needles

I guess you could use a different type of needle, such as a strong darning needle, but sashiko is one of the few types of stitching that is made much easier with the right needle (cross stitch and needlepoint are others). A sashiko needle is long, very rigid and extremely sharp. This is because the stitching technique relies on holding the needle straight and firm while loading the fabric on to the needle, then pulling the thread through, rather than the motion of taking the needle through the static fabric as in traditional quilting. Sashiko needles are easy to find on haberdashery, sewing and quilting websites, and in stores. They come in different lengths and thicknesses, but as they are often available in mixed packs you can try them to see which size and length you prefer.

Threads

Sashiko thread is soft, strong, single-strand cotton that is used double. It is possible to use alternative threads, but to begin with I would suggest using a Japanese brand of sashiko thread (I use Olympus) so that you can get an idea of how it works and the effects you like, before experimenting with other threads. (One word of warning: coton à broder is thinner and much more expensive.) The other advantage of using sashiko threads is that they come in the traditional shades of indigo/white/ecru, as well as a good number of non-classic colours.

Sashiko skeins can be unwound, laid flat and cut at the tied end to make a bundle of approximately 100-cm (39½-in) long single threads. This bundle can then be plaited loosely so that threads can be pulled out as needed and kept tidy at the same time.

Miscellaneous

There is a special type of sashiko thimble that sits at the base of a finger/top of the palm that some stitchers like to use, while others manage without it (I don't use one).

The two designs on pages 25 and 26 can be marked out very easily on a square of fabric using a long ruler (such as a quilter's ruler) and quilter's pencil, or a soluble or fading pen. I used a Japanese chalk wheel (chaco liner) with yellow chalk because I wanted to see how it worked and what was good about it. It's very easy to use but I did find that the chalk lines brushed off very quickly and that I had to redo them frequently.

Resources

If you are inspired to go further with sashiko and want to transfer complex patterns on to fabric, here are some books and suppliers I have found useful.

Susan Briscoe (www.susanbriscoe.co.uk) is an expert on sashiko and has written several books on the subject. She sells patterns and kits through her website and teaches sashiko workshops.

Euro Japan Links (www.eurojapanlinks.com) sells everything you need for sashiko, including Japanese fabrics.

The Cotton Patch in the UK and Purl Soho in the US both carry large ranges of sashiko supplies (but not the authentic fabric).

Stitching technique

In this type of stitching the needle is held still and the fabric is loaded on to it in a kind of pleating motion. Much of the pleasure of sashiko comes from the rhythm involved in this: there is no one way of doing it, so it's best to find a method of working that suits you so that you relax and make all the stitches the same length. It's possible to read a great deal about the ideal number of stitches per inch, which can be anything from four to eight, but the consistency of the stitch length rather than the length itself is more important. There is also debate about the ratio of stitch to gap (or length of top stitch to underside stitch), which is generally agreed to be 3:1 or 3:2. However, each individual stitcher has their own natural length, and you will only find out what works for you by having a go and practising.

When stitching, you should keep the thread a little loose to prevent puckering. Gently pull the fabric widthways after pulling the needle through a set of stitches in order to settle the stitches and make them even. But don't pull too hard as a little extra 'bumpage' creates lovely texture. As you turn a corner, leave a little loop above the corner stitch so that you can ease the stitches gently into place.

When stitching a classic pattern, there is usually a set route across the lines, like a map with directions set out for you so you don't make diversions or get lost. This route-mapping prevents distortion and puckering, and is meant to be very natural and flowing, like good handwriting. Just as everyone has their own signature, so all sashiko is unique and handmade, and even when you are following pre-printed lines, in fact you make the piece your own just by working it in your own unique way.

Starting and finishing

With sashiko a knot is not seen as a heinous stitching crime, and it's quite alright to begin and end with one. In fact, most traditional, hard-wearing sashiko garments and projects are done with knots as these are less likely to come undone than an overstitched stitch, and they do not show through. However, you might prefer to start with a neat overstitch. Needless to say, I love using knots just because they are so often frowned upon elsewhere in the stitching world.

Make the starting knot by tying the two ends of the thread together in a normal knot. Make the finishing knot on the wrong side by taking the thread to the back and wrapping it once around the needle. Then hold the wrapping point while you pull the needle through.

When the work is finished, iron it on the back and not the front.

Free-form sashiko

Although the range of wonderful traditional patterns could keep a stitcher happy for a long time, there are plenty of other ways you can exploit this form of beautifully textured running stitch using thick threads on simple, homely fabrics.

Of course, it is ideal for quilting. The original sashiko technique was used to hold together layers of fabric, and it is quite simple to apply it to a large-scale quilt made with soft, medium-weight fabrics (not lightweight cotton quilting fabrics). Even simple straight lines of quilting look amazing when worked in white or ecru thread on a navy or indigo background, like down-to-earth pinstripes.

Sashiko can also be used whenever lines of running stitch are required. The key is to match the weight of cotton thread to the fabric. So it would make lovely writing or doodling stitching, and is a good way of stitching pictures — as evidenced by the more modern Japanese sashiko designs now available. It can be used to embellish all sorts of textiles such as bags, handkerchiefs, tablecloths, napkins, cushion covers, table runners, hangings and framed pictures.

It's also possible to make up your own free-form sashiko designs, as I have done here.

Furoshiki

This is a traditional Japanese form of gift wrapping using fabric. Simple squares of fabric — printed, plain, stitched — are folded and tied in all sorts of clever ways to wrap objects and, very often, also to provide a handle for carrying all kinds of everyday goods such as clothes, bottles, groceries and bento boxes, as well as gifts. Furoshiki was commonplace before the mid–twentieth century, when people could not afford or did not have access to disposable wrapping; instead they had reusable cloths that could double as useful home textiles and/or gifts.

Furoshiki is now being revived as it is a reusable and environmentally friendly alternative to plastic bags and costly giftwrap. There are many different clever and inventive methods of wrapping, each with its own name, and the results make even the most ordinary object look intriguing when wrapped.

Different–sized squares are used to wrap various articles, although the most common range is from 68—105cm (26³/₄—41¹/₄in).

A square measuring 45—50cm (17³/₄—19³/₄in) is good for small boxes, pieces of stationery and pencil cases, and a 70—75cm (27¹/₂—29¹/₂in) square works for bottles of wine, small cakes in boxes and books. A metre (yard) square is large enough to wrap a bento box or lunch box, or several books, or a boxed gift. It's surprising, though, just how large a square needs to be in proportion to the object to be wrapped, as a lot of fabric is required for the tying.

Warp and Weft Furoshiki

Much as I admire and enjoy looking at complex sashiko patterns, I'm saving them for a later date and concentrating instead on stitching easy, straight, graphic lines that show off the beauty of the stitch and the simplicity of the technique.

This design is worked on soft, indigo–blue Japanese cotton fabric (bought from Susan Briscoe — see Resources on page 21). I wanted to make something that connected to traditional sashiko in terms of fabric, threads and colours, but using a more expansive, large–scale linear pattern that would be straightforward to mark out and stitch. I also wanted to make a piece that could be a furoshiki cloth (see page 23), so big enough to wrap up a box or gift.

Originally I planned to use simple stripes or columns but I then discovered that the sashiko stitching felt and looked slightly different depending on the direction in which I was working, whether it was with the warp or the weft. So I altered my ideas to suit my stitching musings about warp and weft, and took the threads under and over to represent the way fabric is woven (see diagram on page 150).

I created very simple lines with five rows of stitching along each of the warp and weft lines, and two around the edge. I tried to keep all the lines parallel but decided not to worry about it too much — and in fact I would just stick to stitching naturally if I made another version of this design.

The cloth can be used as a wrapping cloth, or as a tablecloth or covering. If made on a smaller scale (very easy to do as you just divide the square into nine squares and mark out the stitching lines), it could be used for a cushion cover. If made on a larger scale, maybe in a rectangle rather than a square, it could be a quilt top.

To make the furoshiki

Any size of square can be used. Simply divide the width by three and mark horizontal and vertical lines accordingly to divide the cloth into nine equal squares. Of course, you could also divide the cloth by five or seven across and down to make more squares.

You will need

A square of fabric (see details on page 20) 3cm (1¼in) larger than the finished piece, whose dimensions should be easily divisible by three: so to make a 75 x 75cm (29½ x 29½in) square you will need to begin with a square of 78 x 78cm (30¾ x 30¾in).

❖ Long ruler
❖ Iron
❖ Pins
❖ Stitching diagram (see page 150)
❖ Fabric marker pen (see page 140)
❖ 2 skeins of cotton sashiko thread used double (I used Olympus), or alternative cotton thread (see details on page 21)
❖ Sashiko needle or very sharp, strong, long needle (see details on page 21)

Finished size: 75 x 75cm (29½ x 29½in).

Making

Fold under, press and pin a double 1.5cm (⅝in) hem around all four edges of the fabric.

Using doubled thread and running stitch (see page 142), stitch two rows of running stitches around the hems.

With a long ruler, check the measurements of the square and divide the edges into thirds. Mark out the lines to create nine smaller squares.

Now stitch the warp and weft pattern taking the threads under at the under and over points.

Pyramid Furoshiki

I wanted to try out fabric bought locally rather than difficult-to-obtain Japanese fabric, and found some very cheap, soft, loosely woven Indian fabric in all sorts of colours. This is a lovely sky-blue and I used ecru sashiko thread to stitch a clean, geometric design of ever-decreasing triangles that make the cloth look like a pyramid seen from above (or it could be a large sea salt crystal). The fabric worked well, which proved that it's quite easy to make substitutions for authentic Japanese fabrics, and the pattern is very easy to mark and stitch.

Once you have divided the square into four equal triangles, it's just a matter of stitching inside them, and the distance between the lines can be as small or as large as you like. I marked lines 7.5cm (3in) apart because I have a long ruler that is 7.5cm (3in) wide; I marked the lines on either side then I went back and stitched lines in between the first lines in two of the triangles. You could add more lines to all four triangles; I left two triangles with fewer lines because I liked the look at that point.

To make the furoshiki

You will need

A square of fabric (see details on page 20) 3cm (1¼in) larger than the finished piece; this piece was 88 x 88cm (34⅝ x 34⅝in) — I would just use whatever suitable square I have to hand rather than worry about being exact.

❖ Long ruler
❖ Iron
❖ Pins
❖ Stitching diagram (see page 150)
❖ Fabric marker pen (see page 140)
❖ 2 skeins of cotton sashiko thread used double (I used Olympus 'natural'), or alternative cotton thread (see details on page 21)
❖ Sashiko needle or very sharp, strong, long needle (see details on page 21)

Finished size: 85 x 85cm (33½ x 33½in)

Making

Fold under, press and pin a double 1.5cm (⅝in) hem around all four edges of the fabric.

Using doubled thread and running stitch (see page 142), stitch two rows of running stitches around the hems.

With a fabric marker, begin by marking and stitching a cross from corner to corner to divide the square into four triangles.

Then simply mark and stitch triangles at equal intervals. You can follow the diagram, or devise your own spacing: the lines can be any distance apart — it depends on the effect you wish to achieve and how much sewing you want to do.

Needlepoint

Needlepoint is one of the simplest forms of stitching and can be mastered in no time at all. There is no need for a frame or any setting up; all you need is some canvas, some wools and a needle.

Above: *Handicraft* (1887) by Yuri Yakovlevich Leman.

Many needlepoint stitchers don't realise that they don't even need a pre-painted canvas or a charted pattern as you can stitch super-simple basic designs of squares, rectangles and stripes to cover the canvas quickly and enjoyably in wonderful colours. If you use a wide-gauge canvas (see page 34), the piece will grow quickly under your fingers; a bright and beautiful needlepoint cushion can be yours in a week, not years. When you have finished, there is no need to seek professional help in stretching and finishing, as this can be done quite easily at home with pins, towels and a spare bit of floor or an ironing board.

A potted history

Needlepoint is a very gentle art. It has a distinguished history and tradition that goes back centuries, but it reached the height of its popularity in the nineteenth century. It is one of the forms of decorative 'fancy work' that is mentioned so frequently in novels by writers such as Elizabeth Gaskell, Charlotte Mary Yonge and the Brontë sisters. Unfortunately it is still often muddled up with tapestry; needlepoint is stitched on a canvas whereas tapestry is woven on a loom, yet even today the wool threads used for needlepoint are called, misleadingly, 'tapestry wools'.

There are many styles of needlepoint, and the one I am drawn to is very high-Victorian Berlin wool work. The appeal of this can be summed up in three very reassuring words: colourful, commercial, charted. When it first arrived in Britain from Germany, the innovative design charts, the brilliant wool colours (made possible by huge progress in dyeing technology and the introduction of new, synthetic dyes in the 1830s) and the commercial approach all took the market by storm, and by the 1850s Berlin wool work had become a national craze.

The trademarks of this wonderfully bright, vibrant, eye-catching style of needlepoint were the dark backgrounds and rich, blowsy, floral designs, made easy to stitch by the supplied printed paper charts (so easy, indeed, that there was, and still is, a degree of sniffiness in some quarters about the artistic merits of this form of needlepoint). The finished pieces were used all over the house: on cushions, firescreens, spectacle cases, bags, footstools, bell pulls, rugs and furniture covers as well as on belts, braces and fancy items for selling at charity bazaars. Many of these can be spotted in the 'genre' paintings of that time, the kind that often feature round-faced, demure, crinolined ladies who were expected to do no more than sit in stuffy, over-furnished rooms and stitch all day. Yet despite all this, I still love the style of Berlin work, its richness, depth of colour and gorgeous designs.

There are similarities between the craze for bright nineteenth-century Berlin wool work and the person who reignited the spark in needlepoint in the last two decades of the twentieth century: Kaffe Fassett. Like the advent of Berlin wool work, Kaffe brought a much-needed boost of colour and excitement to the craft. He, too, was not afraid to reach a wide audience and made needlepoint even easier by selling kits with pre-painted canvases, as well as giving the charts for lush, gorgeous fruit and flower designs in his book *Glorious Needlepoint*.

Since the Kaffe colourburst there has been little to excite in needlepoint, but things are now changing. With the opportunities offered by the internet to reach a specific target audience, we are

Getting started

I first encountered needlepoint via Kaffe Fassett. I stitched a Kaffe cushion design of a huge red parrot tulip on a lime-green background, and I even began one of Elian McCready's enormous, stunning pansy panels, but retired defeated after one corner. Through these I discovered that I love the look of needlepoint and very much enjoy the action and rhythm of stitching, the choosing of colours and seeing how they work next to each other. I also like the fact that needlepoint is portable, light, easy to handle and requires no special equipment, just needle, thread, canvas and scissors. But I was put off by the fact that the projects took an age to complete and that sending my work away to be finished was costly and bothersome. After these two projects I didn't do any needlepoint for a long time, and when I did come back to thinking about it, I realised I needed a very different approach, one that was simpler, more individual and, crucially, less time-consuming. I simplified and simplified until I realised that all I had to do was:
a) buy some canvas and thread
b) make up a pattern
c) start stitching.
The results are the 'One-Week Wonder' and 'Bed of Roses' cushions and a nest of pincushions (see pages 38—40).

seeing some very interesting needlepoint designers setting up websites and offering kits and designs that are far removed from those featuring cats, dogs and cartoon characters. The new style of needlepoint is graphic and bold, with beautiful colours and repeat patterns that are simple to fill in and finish. It is most definitely a good time to revisit needlepoint.

Cushion designs

My first cushion design, the One-Week Wonder (the one in front in the photograph opposite), is based on a traditional patchwork 'sixteen-patch' block in which each square is made up of sixteen squares in two alternating colours. I wanted to prove to myself that a needlepoint cushion cover could be finished in less than a year, so I chose 7 hpi mono canvas (See 'Canvas' on page 34 to find out what this is) and used doubled wool, and made this cushion in exactly seven days. Admittedly I stitched for a great deal of those seven days, but nevertheless it demonstrates that needlepoint is not as time-consuming as so many people think.

The second design is the Bed of Roses cushion cover (behind, in the photograph opposite), which is stitched with a single thread on 10 hpi mono canvas. This is my favourite type of canvas because the work grows nicely and yet the single thread gives it a fine, neat appearance. I found I could fill in up to twenty squares (each seven stitches by seven stitches) in an evening and, as

the design is made up of seventeen squares across and seventeen squares down giving a total of 289 squares, this project took me just over three weeks to stitch (I had a couple of evenings off for good behaviour).

It is called the 'Bed of Roses' because I took my inspiration for the colour scheme from the amazing Queen Mary Rose Garden in London's Regent's Park. I visited the garden early one sunny June morning and was overwhelmed by the vivid pinks, oranges, reds, yellows and lilacs — and by the heady fragrance — and decided to make each square of canvas a representation of a rose, while the grid is worked in a chartreuse green, which is the colour of rose bush leaves.

Canvas

There are two basic types of canvas. Mono (or mono de luxe) is plain, open-weave canvas with a single warp and a single weft thread. It comes in a range of sizes (often referred to as gauge or mesh) and is measured by the number of holes per inch (hpi). Penelope (or double-thread or duo) canvas has two threads in each direction, which means that each hole can be divided into smaller sections to enable much greater delicacy of shading. I use mono canvas because I find it easier to work with and I don't need the extra possibilities of Penelope canvas.

Canvas should be smooth and even; the well-known brand that I use is Zweigart, and the canvas comes in white and 'antique', which is a neutral brownish shade. Antique is best for all but the palest work as white is more likely to show through between threads. I prefer 7 hpi or 10 hpi for speed and density; I like my needlepoint to be fun and enjoyable, and I like to be able to see results after an evening's stitching.

Threads

Although Appleton tapestry wools are generally reckoned to be the finest, they are not easy to find in shops. The wools are available mostly through needlework websites and although I am a fan of internet buying, I find it very difficult to buy from a shade card, even one as lovely as Appleton's (they produce a truly amazing range of colours). So I use Anchor tapestry wools (DMC are just as good), because they are the only ones I can find on the high street. Even these are getting more and more difficult to find, which is quite infuriating because the best way to choose is to pick up lots of skeins and hold them together or lay them out. Then there is the vexing issue of shops allowing shades go out of stock — usually just when you are in the middle of a project. It's worth making a note of the main colours (such as the grid colour), so if you do run out, you can order from a website.

Note: if you are new to needlepoint, be careful not to buy the finer crewel wools for the projects shown here.

How much tapestry wool will I need?

Please note that all tapestry wool requirements are approximate guides. This is because the various stitches and different personal styles use varying amounts of thread (for example, half cross stitch can use up to 25—30 per cent less wool than tent stitch, and some people stitch tightly and some loosely). Also, different brands have different lengths of wool in a skein — for example, Anchor has 10m (11yd) and DMC has 8m (8¾yd).

I work in a very ad hoc way by choosing a bunch of single skeins in ten to fifteen lovely colours that work well together, starting the piece, then going back to buy more when I see how the design is developing and which colours are being used most.

If you want a more precise estimate before you begin, it is worth stitching a sample square using the style, stitch and canvas you intend to use. Note exactly how much wool is used over a number of stitches, then multiply the quantity accordingly.

Needles

The needles to use for needlepoint are called tapestry needles and are widely available. They are thick and blunt, and come in different sizes. Sizes 20 or 22 are fine for using on 7 hpi and 10 hpi canvas.

Frame

These types of straightforward needlepoint projects can be stitched quite easily without a frame (I don't even own a frame). This has the advantage of making the work portable, plus it means you can stitch while sitting comfortably in a chair rather than hunched over a frame.

Stitches

Although there are many different decorative needlepoint stitches, you only need one basic diagonal stitch to stitch these projects. There are three versions of this stitch:

Continental tent stitch (see page 143) gives good coverage and is the stitch I use. If you prefer working in one direction more than the other (say, from right to left), you can turn the canvas after every row so you're always working in your preferred direction.

Half cross stitch (see page 145) uses less wool but can leave the canvas feeling light, plus pale canvas can show through the finished work as this stitch does not give the best coverage.

The stitch you choose is a matter of personal preference and whichever is easier for you. Before you embark on a large piece of needlepoint, it's best to practise a few rows of stitching in each direction in order to develop your style and rhythm. But I guarantee it won't take more than an hour for you to pick up all the skills you need.

Designing

It is completely possible to simply thread a needle and start stitching. But if you want to make plans and designs, the best way is to sketch out ideas on graph paper with a scale that matches the gauge of the canvas you are using. This graph paper is easy to find on the internet (try www.stitchpoint.com) and can be printed out. Then all you have to do is sketch, colour in or design a chart in which one square represents a single stitch.

Preparing canvas

Before you begin stitching, mark the main outline of the area to be stitched with permanent marker pen so that you can cut the canvas with a generous allowance around the edges. Canvas frays quite easily once it is handled, plus you need extra for stretching and blocking, so allow for a minimum 7.5cm (3in) margin all around (I prefer to have a more generous margin).

Bind the edges with masking tape to prevent them fraying and to stop the tapestry wools catching on the ends of the canvas threads.

Starting stitching

For a cushion, the finished piece needs to be one of the standard cushion sizes, so it's worth buying the pad first and measuring it. Alternatively, you can simply create a lovely piece of work and stuff it with polyester stuffing if it turns out not to be a standard size.

Whether you are following one of the charts here, or your own design, or just working in an ad hoc way, begin in the top right-hand corner and work your way across the canvas, spreading out from the corner as you go along. I'm not too rigid about a method, and often leave out/fill in squares until/when I see where a certain colour will look good. With the Bed of Roses cushion I didn't stitch the grid first, but this could be done and the squares filled in afterwards.

To start the first length of wool, bring the needle through to the front, leaving a 1—2cm ($^3/_8$—$^3/_4$in) tail of wool at the back. Hold this tail horizontally at the back of the canvas and stitch over it as you work the first row. For all subsequent lengths, run the wool through the back of the stitches recently worked and adjacent to the new start point. When finishing, simply run the wool through the back of the stitches on a recently worked row of the same colour. Cut any loose ends. Do not leave any long ends at the back of the work as they will invariably become tangled up with your stitching. Do not use knots as they tend to eventually work their way through the canvas and appear on the front.

It's worth stitching one extra border row right around the edge of the design; it'll be useful when you make up the cushion (see 'Making Up the Cushion', opposite).

Stretching and blocking

If you stitch without a frame, the finished piece will probably be distorted and will need to be stretched and blocked into shape. This has often been seen as the province of the professionals with their special equipment, but in fact it's very easy to block your canvas at home. All you need are stainless-steel pins — I use long, strong quilting pins (avoid anything that will rust and leave a mark) — a soft, absorbent towel, a tea towel or piece of calico, and a flat surface that can hold pins. I use an area of carpeted floor and I push the pins into the underlay to hold the canvas securely. If you are stretching a small piece, an ironing board will suffice.

Lay out a colourfast towel with a piece of calico or a tea towel on top (nothing with any colour that may run) on the flat surface you are using. With a spray water bottle, damp sponge or tea towel, dampen the top side of the work until it feels damp on the back and not just on the surface, but do not soak it.

Gently pull the edges of the work until the sides are straight, or as straight as you can get them. You may want to use a paper template of the finished cushion size or a ruler or, even better, a large quilter's ruler to check that the sides and corners are straight.

Now, pin the canvas firmly to the surface/carpet, putting the pins in at an angle to keep them in place and pinning close to the edge of the work, but without touching the stitching. Leave until the work is completely dry, which will take two to four days depending on the ambient temperature.

Your work may need two blocking sessions to make it completely straight. It is sometimes easier to do this than to aim for perfection the first time around.

Backing fabrics

All the needlepoint projects here are backed with velvet for contrasting depth of colour and beautiful texture; the cushions have cotton velvet backs and the pincushions have silk velvet backs. Many needlepoint cushions have piping around the edge, but I didn't use any as I wanted mine to be as unfussy and manageable as possible.

Making up
the cushion

When the piece has been stretched, trim the bare canvas margins to 2cm (³⁄₄in) — leave a wider margin on the side that is going to be left open to insert the cushion pad before sewing up; I would leave at least 10cm (4in) and trim later if need be. Remember that the canvas frays very easily when cut so don't trim it until you are ready to make up the cushion, and always handle it carefully.

Pin the backing fabric to the needlepoint, right sides facing. Machine-sew carefully around three sides, sewing between the extra outer row of stitching (see Starting Stitching) and the next row in.

Trim the edges if necessary and turn the cover right side out. Insert the cushion pad or stuffing. Fold in and pin the edges of the fourth side together and hand-stitch it closed.

Further inspiration
and books

There is not a great deal in the way of contemporary needlepoint inspiration in books. Indeed, very little has been published on the subject in recent years, and existing books tend to focus on Art and Crafts style or the lushly gorgeous style of the 1980s/1990s. However, I still find *Glorious Needlepoint* by Kaffe Fassett (1987) to be one of the best sources of ideas, inspiration and useful techniques.

Unsurprisingly, there is more inspiration on the internet these days, where young, modern designers with a fresh, graphic approach are writing about needlepoint and selling their designs and kits on websites. My favourites are Emily Peacock (www.emilypeacock.com) and Felicity Hall (www.felicityhall.co.uk).

To make the Bed of Roses cushion cover

You will need

- ❖ 5—6 x 10m (11yd) skeins of tapestry wool (see details on page 34) for the grid (I used Anchor shade 9274)
- ❖ Approximately 17—18 x 10m (11yd) skeins of tapestry wool in assorted colours for the 'roses' (I used an assortment that includes Anchor shades 8438, 8200, 9534, 8492, 8124, 8486, 8456, 8256, 8156, 8094, 8232, 8452, 8434, 8098, 8218, 8214, 8442, 8398, 8018, 8434, 8488, 8528, 8352, 8426, 8194, 8496, 8436, 8488, 8436, 8304, 8196, 8306, 8212, 8116)
- ❖ Piece of 10 hpi mono canvas (see details on page 34) 8—10cm (3—4in) larger all around than the finished cushion size
- ❖ Size 20 or 22 tapestry needle (see details on page 35)
- ❖ Piece of backing fabric (see details on page 37) measuring approximately 45 x 45cm (17³⁄₄ x 17³⁄₄in)
- ❖ 35 x 35cm (13³⁄₄ x 13³⁄₄in) cushion pad
- ❖ Needle and sewing thread for sewing up

Finished size: 35 x 35cm (13³⁄₄ x 13³⁄₄in).

Making

Stitch the cover following the instructions on pages 36—37. The grid is one stitch wide and each small square is seven stitches by seven stitches.

To make the One-Week Wonder cushion cover

You will need

- ❖ Approximately 26 x 10m (11yd) skeins of tapestry wool (see details on page 34) in a mix of bright, vivid colours, or whatever colour scheme you prefer. (I used Anchor leftovers and oddments with a rule of thumb of one dark and one light shade per 'sixteen–patch' square)
- ❖ A piece of 7 hpi mono canvas (see details on page 34) 8—10cm (3—4in) larger all around than the finished cushion size
- ❖ Size 20 or 22 tapestry needle (see details on page 35)
- ❖ Piece of backing fabric (see details on page 37) measuring approx 35 x 35cm (13¾ x 13¾in)
- ❖ 30 x 30cm (12 x 12in) cushion pad
- ❖ Needle and sewing thread for sewing up

Finished size: 30 x 30cm (12 x 12in).

Making

Stitch the cover following the instructions on pages 36—37. Each small square is five stitches by five stitches. Each large block is four squares by four squares, worked in two colours.

Spring Greens Pincushions

I also made a few pincushions with leftover canvas and threads in a range of leafy greens and limey yellows, just for the fun of stitching something in an evening. I used the same basic grid pattern as in the Bed of Roses cushion (see page 38), and made a 'nest' of pincushions that range from five squares by five squares, to two squares by two squares. (I wanted to make a tiny, single-square version but it proved too difficult to turn right side out.) The little projects allowed me to experiment with different grid colours and to see how they alter the look of the piece. (If you need a quick-to-make gift for a keen sewer, I recommend one of these.)

To make the pincushions

You will need

❖ Small amounts of tapestry wools (see details on page 34) in various colours (I used Anchor shades 9116, 9196, 9502, 9120, 9282, 9656, 9154, 9602)
❖ Piece of 10 hpi mono canvas (see details on page 34) 4cm (1¹/₂in) larger all around than the finished size
❖ Size 20 or 22 tapestry needle (see details on page 35)
❖ Backing fabric (see details on page 37) 4cm (1¹/₂in) larger all around than the finished size
❖ Small amount of stuffing
❖ Needle and sewing thread for sewing up

Finished size: whatever you want.

Making

Stitch the pincushions following the instructions on pages 36—37. The grid is one stitch wide and each small square is seven stitches by seven stitches.

Shade numbers

The shade numbers given are for Anchor tapestry wools, so do remember that different brands will have different reference numbers (if you want guidance, some websites have DMC/Anchor conversion charts). You do not have to use Anchor wools — just use whatever tapestry wools are available to you in the colours you like.

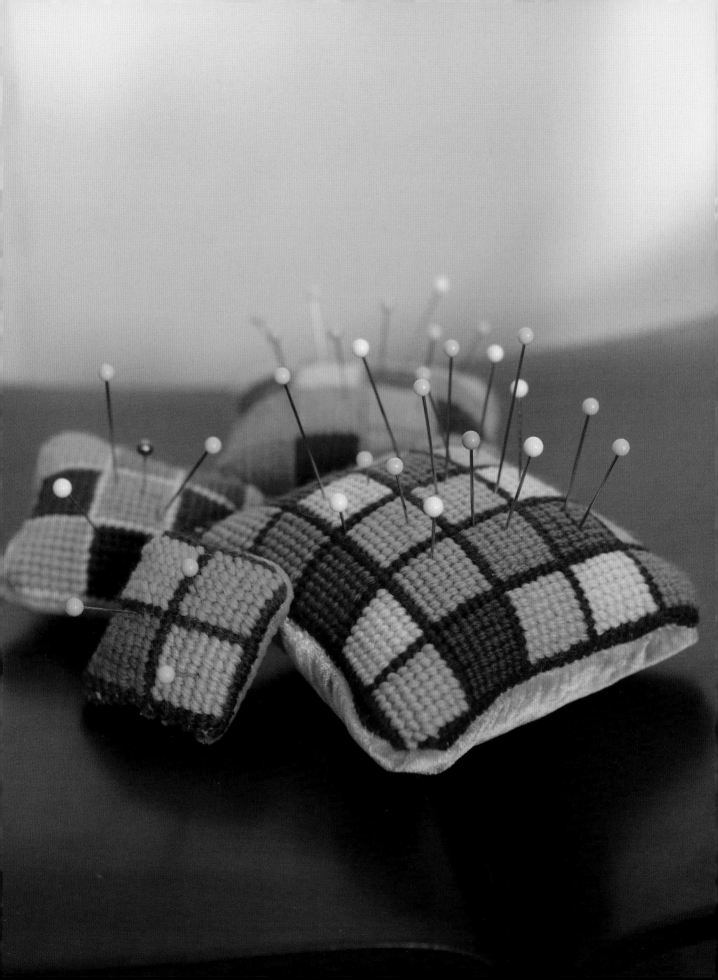

Seasonal kantha

Although kantha is a very traditional form of stitching in parts of India, it's still relatively new in the West. But with increased interest in, and availability of, beautiful kantha quilts and stitched articles from Bangladesh and West Bengal, this is beginning to change.

The appeal of kantha is very easy to understand: it takes the simplest stitch, running stitch, and exploits its possibilities in all sorts of creative and inventive ways. It is a very unselfconsciously visible style of stitching and, like Japanese sashiko (see page 16), it challenges our Western perceptions of a hierarchy of stitches in which running stitch is usually seen as the lowest of the low.

Kantha was originally used to stitch together pieces and layers of old saris to make simple quilts, cloths, bedspreads, covers and mats. The base is usually a thin white sari fabric (soft old cotton pillowcases and sheets make good substitutes) whose surface is covered with running stitch in all sorts of traditional patterns, flowers, animals, birds and geometric shapes, customarily worked in red and blue. The apparent naivety and density of the stitching create a variety of textures and swirls, waves and wrinkles, ripples and ridges that make the resulting cloth hard-wearing and decorative.

It's a form of stitching still practised by women in rural areas of India, but now that there is growing interest from textile tourists, contemporary kantha is becoming less traditional in terms of motifs and colours. There is also a trend towards simple kantha stitching on printed backgrounds, instead of the typically plain, neutral cottons. These are produced for the Western market, and even though purists may object, I find their mix of dense running stitch and lovely colours very seductive, and I enjoy and admire the way that kantha is evolving in order to sustain its development and to continue its fascinating stitching history.

Kantha-inspired designs

I took the kantha elements I like most — running stitch and soft fabrics — and made two quilts that could loosely be called 'kantha', although 'kantha-inspired' is probably more accurate.

True kantha is made using a huge range of patterns and motifs all worked in running stitch. Even though these have been passed down from generation to generation of women, the wonderful thing is that no two kanthas are alike, as the stitcher works intuitively, with her own stitching style and signature, playing with colour and placement, and using running stitch in inventive ways to cover the fabric. So, in the same spirit of reinvention and adaptation, I decided to make up my own kantha style, using cotton fabrics with large-scale patterns (as seen in the new 'kantha' quilts being made in India for overseas markets), colourful threads and huge amounts of running stitch to create texture. It's not at all authentic, but it's very easy and enjoyable stitching: meditative, simple, and plain, but made interesting by the stitches and the colours. I made two of my 'kantha' quilts, one for summer and one for winter.

Exploring kantha

As kantha is still a mainly undiscovered type of stitching, there is very little in the way of available reference material and resources. A few dealers and a number of companies sell the Westernised versions of kanthas, and the Philadelphia Museum of Art (www.philamuseum.org) has an excellent selection of traditional kantha quilts on its website.

Lynn Setterington (www.lynnsetterington.co.uk) is a UK expert and kantha stitcher who has developed a very contemporary and beautiful style of kantha quilting. She also teaches kantha workshops.

The Art of Kantha Embroidery by Niaaz Zaman (University Press, Bangladesh, 1995).

Kantha: The Embroidered Quilts of Bengal from the Sheldon and Jill Bonovitz Collection and the Stella Kramrisch Collection of the Philadelphia Museum of Art by Danielle Mason et al. (Yale University Press, 2009).

Right: Sampler of kantha stitches.

Summer Kantha Quilt

This summer kantha quilt is an opportunity to use a lovely fabric design, a piece of fabric you adore, have perhaps been hoarding, and don't really want to cut into, something exciting that would work well when covered with running stitch. (Big Indian or Mexican-style florals work wonderfully well, while small, fussy designs fight for attention with the stitches.) Most traditional kanthas are 'whole cloth' quilts: they are made with just one piece of fabric (or several pieces of the same fabric), so using one main design plus extras, as I have done here, is a variation on the theme. The alternative would be to use completely plain fabric and show off the stitches even more.

Fabrics

I bought two 2-metre (2¼-yd) lengths of 106-cm (42-in) wide cotton quilting fabric as the main pieces, one for the top and one for the back, both in a chocolate brown/pale blue/pink colour scheme. I then added an extra column of fabric down one edge using an offcut of the fabric on the other side of the quilt, together with a couple more fabrics. This makes the quilt totally reversible, though for clarity in explaining how it was made, I'll call the blue and pink floral side (Kaffe Fassett's 'Big Blooms') the top, and the brown-with-small-flowers side (Kaffe Fassett's 'Guinea Flower') the back.

I widened both the front and back with strips of three fabrics from Denyse Schmidt's 'Katie Jump Rope' collection, as well as the offcut piece from the opposite side of the quilt. I placed the additional sections to the left of the main fabric because I find my eye naturally reads a quilt like writing, or at least that is the way I want to guide the eye. The binding is 'Aboriginal Dots' by Kaffe Fassett.

Threads

Although standard six-strand embroidery thread is widely available in hundreds of colours, I find it difficult to use for quilting and prefer cotton perlé. If you have never used it before, it is a complete revelation as it is smooth and hardly ever tangles. It has a fabulous sheen, is a joy to stitch with, and comes in wonderful squat spools. It is loosely cabled so it doesn't untwist, and it sits slightly proud of the surface thus giving added texture.

Since kantha involves a lot of repetitive stitching, you might as well enjoy yourself with good threads and sustain your interest with different colours. I took the fabrics I was going to use to a shop and chose the thread colours there — all are Finca Cotton Perlé 8. It is amazing how even a mostly pastel fabric can swallow stitches in paler colours, and I found I needed to choose quite boldly, picking out the brighter and deeper colours in the design.

Stitching

I started stitching in multiples of three rows, and started a colour change pattern moving from light to dark and back again, but soon forgot it, relaxed into the stitching and simply chose the next colour according to what I thought would look good. I stitched horizontal lines on the main section, and vertical lines on the side section (sets of three rows of the same colour on the horizontal, and sets of two rows on the vertical). I found it quite easy to keep the lines straight by following points in the design and/or any seams, but stitching lines can be marked in advance if necessary (see page 140). My stitches and spacing are much larger and wider than true kantha, but I wanted this to be a reasonably fast project.

Filling

I used 100 per cent cotton wadding with scrim to hold the fabric more securely, but any quilt filling would work. Alternatively, use a layer or two of recycled cotton fabric.

To make the summer quilt

You will need

- ❖ Two pieces of lightweight cotton fabric (see details on page 46), each measuring 200 x 106cm (79 x 42in)
- ❖ Approximately 65 x 106cm (25½ x 42in) in total of three lightweight cotton fabrics (see details on page 46)
- ❖ Tape measure
- ❖ Fabric marker
- ❖ Scissors
- ❖ Quilter's pins
- ❖ Sewing machine
- ❖ Sewing thread
- ❖ Piece of wadding (see details on page 46) measuring approximately 168 x 140cm (66 x 55in)
- ❖ Embroidery threads (see details on page 46)
- ❖ Embroidery needle
- ❖ Piece of lightweight cotton fabric (see details on page 46) measuring 106 x 40cm (42 x 15¾in)
- ❖ Sewing needle

Finished size: 152 x 128cm (60 x 50½in).

Making

The measurements given are those that I used, but you can of course adjust them, though the back should always be about 8—10cm (3—4in) larger all around than the top.

Making sure the edges are square and straight, cut the main fabric for the top to measure 162 x 106cm (64 x 42in) and the main fabric for the back to measure 178 x 106cm (70 x 42in).

Machine-sew pieces of the offcut top and back fabrics and the two extra fabrics together to make the strips for widening the top and back. I used the back offcut on the top and vice versa (see page 46). Pin pieces right sides together and, taking a 1cm (⅜in) seam allowance (use this seam allowance throughout), machine-sew them. The strip for the top needs to be 162 x 27cm (64 x 10½in) and the strip for the back needs to be 178 x 37cm (70 x 14½in). Press all the seam allowances in the same direction.

Pin the top strip right sides together to one long edge of the top and machine-sew the seam. Sew the back strip to the back in the same way. Press the seams towards the main piece.

Assemble the quilt by making a quilt 'sandwich'. Place the backing fabric right side down on a flat surface. Put the wadding on top, and smooth the backing and the wadding to remove any wrinkles. Put the quilt top on top, making sure it is centred and square on the backing and wadding. Smooth it again to remove any wrinkles and bumps. Pin the layers together with a pin every 15cm (6in) across and down the sandwich.

Work running stitch through all layers across the quilt (see page 142). You can follow the patterns I used or create your own designs.

Trim the edges so that the backing and wadding are the same size as the top. Bind the edges of the quilt with fabric strips. There are various ways of binding edges and the method I use is quite simple.

To bind a quilt

Cut 5-cm (2-in) wide strips of fabric, either on the straight grain or on the bias. Making diagonal seams, join enough strips to make one long strip that will fit right around the edge of your quilt, plus a little extra for the overlap.

Cut the ends of the long strip at a 45-degree angle and turn under and press a 5mm (¼in) hem on each end. Wrong sides together, fold the strip in half lengthways and press it.

On the right side of the quilt and starting in the middle of one edge, pin one end of the folded binding strip to the edge of the quilt, with right sides together and the raw edges of the strip aligned with the edge of the quilt.

Set the sewing machine to a medium straight stitch and, taking a 5mm (¼in) seam allowance, sew the strip to the quilt along one edge. Stop 5mm (¼in) from the end, reverse to secure the threads, then cut them.

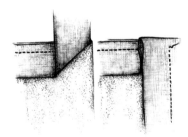

Fold the binding back over itself at a 45-degree angle, so that the loose strip is trailing away from the quilt at right

angles to the part that is sewn on. Pin the inner edge of the fold to keep it in place.

Without distorting the diagonal fold, fold the binding down over itself so that there is a straight fold aligned with the first edge of the quilt, and one raw edge of the loose strip is aligned with the next edge of the quilt to be bound.

Starting where the last line of machining ended, sew the binding to this edge of the quilt.

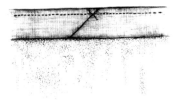

Repeat this process at all four corners. When you reach the beginning of the binding strip, lay the free end over it and complete the sewing.

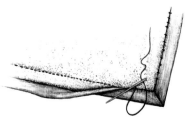

Turn the folded edge of the binding over the edge of the quilt and to the back. Arrange it so that it just covers the line of machine stitching and hand-sew it in place. As you reach each corner, mitre it neatly.

Winter Kantha Quilt

This is a quilt with a high snuggle factor because of its woollen back and cotton wadding filling. It is very warm and comforting, and I like the contrast of textures and the way the stitches look different on the patterned top and the plain back. Indeed, it's a real camper van quilt; it's very sturdy and if you used a darker coloured wool fabric (maybe an old blanket) on the back, it could be used as a rug.

Fabrics

I wanted to show off a few deeply coloured and extravagantly floral fabrics and lots of running stitch, and at the same time experiment with a warm, wool backing for a change. On the top I used four full-width, 50cm (20in) panels of 106-cm (42-in) wide cotton quilting fabric (but these could be half-yard lengths, or any shape or size you like). I chose lacquer-red fabrics with big flowers, which were as close as I could get to a Japanese kimono feel. Three are by Martha Negley and one is a Heather Bailey design. I went for scarlet red and limey-green threads for the stitching and I put a simple woven off-white wool fabric on the back so the quilt had the feel of a warm, weighty blanket. The binding is Kaffe Fassett's 'Arts and Crafts' in lime.

Filling and stitching

Initially I stitched the top and bottom together without a filling, but in the absence of tacking the fabrics wouldn't hold together well and it was difficult to stitch the straight lines freehand. I should perhaps have marked and tacked the quilt top, but I prefer a more relaxed approach. So I added a layer of cotton quilt wadding between the top and back and started stitching the three layers together, something that proved to be much harder on my hands and fingers than I'd anticipated. I had to use a sashiko needle (see page 21) for its sharpness, strength and large eye for the thick thread, and stitched four equally spaced bands of running stitch, each between 15—20cm (6-8in) wide across the width of the quilt, covering approximately half of each section of fabric. This creates plenty of texture but also lots of contrast and allows the beautiful designs to be fully appreciated.

To make the winter quilt

You will need

❖ Four pieces of lightweight cotton fabric (see details, left), each measuring 106 x 50cm (42 x 20in)
❖ Piece of wool fabric measuring approximately 190 x 127cm (75 x 50in)
❖ Tape measure
❖ Fabric marker
❖ Scissors
❖ Quilter's pins
❖ Sewing machine
❖ Sewing thread
❖ Piece of wadding (see details, left) measuring 190 x 127cm (75 x 50in)
❖ Embroidery threads (see details on page 46 and left)
❖ Embroidery needle
❖ Piece of lightweight cotton fabric (see details, left) measuring 106 x 40cm (42 x 15¾in)
❖ Sewing needle

Finished size: 165 x 102cm (65 x 40in).

Making

Trim the edges and selvedges of the four cotton fabrics and ensure they are all of equal width. Pin two pieces right sides together along a long edge and, taking a 1cm (³/₈in) seam allowance (use this seam allowance throughout), machine-sew the seam. Repeat to sew all four pieces together to make a quilt top measuring approximately 170 x 106cm (67 x 42in).

Follow the instructions given for the summer quilt to make up and bind this winter quilt: stitching details are on pages 46—49.

Fabric flower arrangements

There is nothing more uplifting than a bunch of fresh tulips or daffodils in a simple vase, and nothing more luxurious than a huge indoor explosion of scented blooms. But I don't just enjoy real flowers, I also love them on fabrics. It is possible to find every kind of flower on fabric, and they can all be used to make long-lasting, hand-stitched pictures.

I am calling this section 'fabric flower arrangements' rather than 'appliqué', because I am not terribly fond of the images associated with that word. In my experience, appliqué is shorthand for traditional designs that require immaculate stitching and technique. The word 'appliqué' is from the French verb 'to apply' and in the context of stitching it simply means to apply one piece of fabric to another, which is what I am doing here in a very enjoyable, but not very traditional, way. I am not over-concerned with straightness, neat edges, finishing and flatness, but I am more interested in building up a framed fabric flower arrangement with lovely fabrics and simple and colourful stitches. If this is appliqué, then it is very relaxed appliqué.

It's absorbing and therapeutic, and you can create framed arrangements that are as generously extravagant or as carefully controlled as you please.

Inspiration

A few years ago I did a workshop with Janet Bolton, a well-known artist who makes unique 'textile pictures' using simple, everyday fabrics and tiny details in a delicate, folk art, naïve style that is unmistakably hers. Each of her pictures tells a little story and has a very natural honesty about it. Although the visible, simple stitching looks easy, it is impossible to copy her work as it is the embodiment of a totally personal technique and way of stitching. Every time someone attempts to make a 'Janet Bolton' — and plenty of people try — something is missing. So for me, the biggest, most significant lesson of the workshop was that it is far better to put yourself into your stitching than to try to copy someone else, and this is how I came to make my flower arrangements.

Arranging flowers

At that first workshop, I saw what Janet made, and decided to have a go at a cotton picture inspired by her style. The result was fine, but totally uninspiring and very ordinary. It was over-stitched, over-thought out and overcrowded, and I was disappointed. So on the second day I decided to use Janet's inspirational words and her basic principles of simple stitches and careful placement to make a picture that reflected my own tastes and pleased me. The result was my first-ever fabric flower arrangement — my auricula picture (the photograph top right).

I surrounded myself with fabrics I liked (the best way to start), decided on a background, and started cutting out shapes and details. Instead of creating flowers and pictures from scratch, I decided to exploit the flowers and leaves that already existed on a fabric, and I cut out the auricula flowers from a Kaffe Fassett design.

Auriculas are one of my favourite flowers; they come in all sorts of beautiful, strange colours but are very tricky to grow so I thought it would be nice to have an immortal auricula arrangement instead. As the flowers are quite rare and deeply coloured, I chose equally special and richly coloured silk rather than cotton for most of the piece, and I also did all the stitching with some silk threads I'd treated myself to but never used. (A small project like this is ideal for using the tiny amounts of special threads, fabrics and beads that you've been hoarding away, while also wishing they could be seen.)

Making the auricula picture was pure pleasure. It didn't seem like hard work and there were no rules or instructions; all I had to do was cut out, play, position, pin and stitch. Every time I looked at it subsequently, I wondered why I hadn't made more. But workshops have their

own magic and it's often difficult to recreate that energy and spark of creativity once you are back at home. But one day when I was sorting out fabrics for a quilt, I found myself looking at the wonderful flowers that appear on so many patchwork/quilting fabrics and, like a child, I wanted to cut them out and make them into a picture.

The auricula piece was small, but I realised that my new picture was going to be much bigger and, actually, much more me. (The interesting thing about watching other people at Janet's workshops is that everyone seems to have their own natural scale of work. Some made exquisite pictures measuring only 10 x 10cm (4 x 4in), while others found themselves covering all the workspace in front of them. (Lesson: don't start with a plan, but just let your eye and hand guide you.)

I made two exuberant flower arrangements (more Constance Spry than Japanese ikebana), inspired by the fabrics and then named for the artist whose look they have. The Matisse picture is so called because of the rather relaxed, stylised look, but also because I adore the deep jades and rich, chalky pinks that recur in his paintings. The second is in the Henri Rousseau style of upright, beautifully arranged and rather stylised but colourful, extravagant flowers. Both are made with the same techniques, but as the fabric frame can be altered to suit the picture, each has a slightly different frame style.

Matisse Flowers

With this arrangement, as with real flower arrangements, I began with the flowers. I chose a simple, relaxed bunch of one variety ('bubble' flowers, not usually found in gardens), decided on a suitable 'vase', then looked for leaves and cut out one set of 'real' leaves and one set of more abstract leaves from a different fabric.

The flowers on this piece have raw edges, that is to say, they are not turned under before stitching. This was the result of a happy accident; I cut them out to the finished size when first playing with the fabric and then I liked them as they were. It's really only possible to leave the edges raw like this if you know the piece isn't going to be used on something that will get a lot of wear (for example, on a cushion or quilt), as they would fray.

The frame is made of two fabrics from the same Echino range; the stripes stand out and frame one half, while the spots part of the frame continues the background and keeps the space open and airy.

Fabrics

I used Echino spots for the background and the stripy frame is an Echino stripe. The abstract pattern leaves are made with Alexander Henry's 'Birdsong' and the green leaves were cut out of 'Embroidered Leaf' by Kaffe Fassett. The flowers come from Kaffe Fassett's 'Bubble Flower', and the vase was made from an oddment of vintage fabric.

Rousseau Flowers

Again, I started with the blooms. This was to be a much more formal, mixed arrangement but with no care for reality or seasonality — I just wanted a large, full, exuberant display. So I cut out all sorts of flowers, large and small, which I thought might work together and played for quite a while arranging them, overlapping them, adding little flowers here and there. The arrangement was so full that I decided to keep the vase plain and used a leftover piece of silk.

What made all the difference was the background. Initially, I used a plain cream background with a woven stripe, but it was too flat and uninspiring. So I tried several other fabrics until I saw that the spotty one was just right. I'd been avoiding spots on the grounds of repetition (I didn't want to duplicate the Matisse arrangement), but maybe I've stumbled upon a flower–arranging truth that all flowers look great against spots?

The frame is made of two fabrics that contrast with the background and pick out colour themes. A simple lilac silk and a brilliantly coloured Martha Negley print bring rich colours and create a very definite frame.

All the edges of the pieces of fabric are turned under in this arrangement.

Fabrics

I used silk for the vase, Martha Negley's 'Maples' and lilac silk for the frame, and Kaffe Fassett's 'Spots' for the background. The flowers are all cut from Kaffe Fassett fabrics, including 'Gazania', 'Flower Basket', 'Big Blooms' and 'Flower Lattice'. The leaves are cut from the leaves on Kaffe Fassett's 'Chard' and leafy parts of 'Flower Lattice'.

Making your own fabric flower arrangement

What is so enjoyable about cutting out and making pictures is that they start with basic ideas, but can soon turn into something that is yours and yours alone. Just like Janet Bolton's artworks, my pictures should not be copied slavishly but should be regarded as a starting point, a way of developing your confidence to get out the fabrics and the scissors and to create your own individual and unique style. This is a great way to use up small and precious scraps of fabrics, but the final dimensions of your piece can be as tiny or as large-scale as you like.

You will need
- ❖ Fabrics (see details below)
- ❖ Threads (see details below)
- ❖ Beads and/or sequins to embellish (optional extras)
- ❖ Sewing needle
- ❖ Pins

Fabrics
Flowers: an assortment of scraps of floral fabrics. Dress or quilt-weight cotton, linens and silks are best as they are thin enough to turn under without creating bulky edges. eQuilter and Glorious Color (see Resources, page 158) have enormous ranges of floral fabrics. My favourite floral designers are Philip Jacobs, Kaffe Fassett and Martha Negley.

Leaves: use either leaves printed on fabrics or cut out fabric in leaf shapes.

Vase: any lightweight fabric you like (I used silk for one and vintage cotton for the other). This can be printed or plain or woven, and can be stitched on later.

Background: the background is double thickness, so use your chosen fabric on top and any lightweight cotton/calico underneath to add weight. I discovered, while making mine, that spots are ideal; eQuilter and many quilting fabric shops and websites have sections devoted to spots and dots. I particularly like spotty fabrics produced by Lecien and by Kaffe Fassett.

Frame: the frame can be made from strips of just one fabric or any mix of fabrics. If you have a tiny amount of a fabric that works, use it — position it, for example, near a corner to add interest. The frame can be a simple, single frame all around, or it can be layered underneath and/or overlapped. Choose a few fabrics that contrast with the background and highlight colours in the flowers.

Threads
The whole piece is hand-sewn and you can use basic all-purpose sewing cotton to stitch the frame and background together, but I prefer to see all the stitches in this piece and use decorative threads throughout. I used cotton embroidery threads (DMC and Anchor, two or three strands) for the cotton Matisse picture. But for most of the silk auricula picture and in places on the Rousseau Flowers picture (such as the silk vase), I used silk threads. Working with silk thread on silk fabrics is a real treat, and if you are making just a small piece or stitching a small area, it keeps the cost down. Silk threads are increasingly widely available from both big manufacturers and small producers. My favourites are the gorgeous Mulberry Silks (see Resources, page 158).

Making
Some people may prefer to make the background and frame first, and then add the flowers, but I find that the best way to begin is with the flowers and leaves. Pull out all your floral fabrics and have a look at the flowers: not all will work when cut out as some overlap too much in a design and don't appear as full blooms, and others look too abstract when taken out of context. If you need inspiration, look at postcards of favourite paintings, or paintings in books and galleries, or on internet art sites such as the brilliant Bridgeman Art Library (www.bridgemanart.com).

You might want to get cutting and arranging immediately, but do remember that if you plan to turn the edges under you need to cut out all your pieces LARGER than the finished size to allow for this. Allow 2—5mm (⅛—¼in), depending on how you feel about tucking under and stitching. I find my turning-under works better with a slightly larger allowance, but some stitchers can turn under very successfully with very little allowance. If you plan to leave the edges of the flowers/leaves raw, simply cut out the pieces to the finished size.

Once you have cut out your flowers and leaves, try different arrangements with them on what you think might be a suitable background. If you happen upon an arrangement you like but need to experiment with the background, take a photo to remind yourself of the positions of the flowers before you remove them.

Next choose the fabric for the vase, and the shape of the vase. Both of mine are slender, upright shapes, but yours can be any shape.

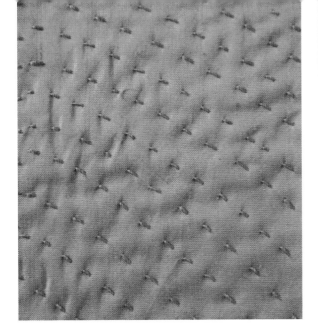

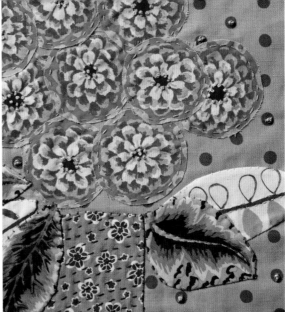

Now make the decision on the background fabric. The background needs to be double thickness (the frame is double or, in places, triple fabric), which gives something relatively strong and flat to stitch on. The second, backing layer can be any fabric — it does not have to match the top as it will not show. The double thickness also adds to the texture by plumping up the stitches. You could also use a thicker, furnishing-weight fabric (as I have done for the Matisse arrangement), with a piece of plain cotton or calico as backing.

Decide on the size of the background. Place the flowers, leaves and vase in position on the background and work out the best size — do you want lots of space around the flowers or a compact look — by turning the edges over to the back until you are happy. Add the backing layer of fabric underneath and trim to size. Photograph it if necessary before removing the arrangement so that you can stitch the background and frame.

Make the frame by using generous strips of fabric (they can be trimmed later) folded over and/or under the edges of the background fabric: this technique is very easy — it just requires folding and stitching into place. Experiment with different fabrics in the frame, adding small pieces to create interest. Tuck the fabric strips under at the corners, and add extra sections or layers of framing if you like: a small peek of a layer of different fabric or an inner frame adds richness and detail. Each edge can be different and can be made of more than one fabric, but it is best to keep to a similar weight of fabric throughout.

Now stitch the frame on to the background. Make sure you pin, pin, pin before stitching so that nothing moves out of place while you handle the fabric, though a little wonkiness adds to the handmade character of the piece. I use small running stitches and the occasional cross stitch and I vary the colour of the threads, but there are no rules about which stitches or colours to use.

Iron the vase and the flowers before pinning them on to the background. Arrange the flowers once more and pin every single piece in place.

Stitch the flowers on to the background, turning the edges where necessary. Choose whatever stitches you like. Use overstitch or close-to-the-edge running stitch for the flowers, and fill in with running stitch to outline, highlight, or add surface interest. French knots look good in the centres of flowers.

Overstitch the outer edges of the vase and add decorative stitching to the main part to create lines and patterns, and to keep it flat.

If you like, you can add a sprinkling of beads to any part of the piece to finish it. I added a little aura of sparkly beads around my arrangements.

Mounting and framing

A flower arrangement such as this is too fragile to be used in a quilt or as a cushion cover (though a sturdier version would be fine) and is best mounted and framed.

Use a heavy board for mounting. Allow for as much or as little space around the piece as you like, and place the finished piece on top. When you are happy with the placement, make marks on the board at the four corners and at the middle points of the edges by pressing through the fabric with a sharp needle so that you can see where to make holes for stitching the piece to the board.

With a strong, sharp needle, make two holes at each corner and at intervals around the edge and stitch the piece on using a strong thread, such as quilting thread, used double so you can pull tightly to get the picture to lie flat. Make sure the stitches are tiny and don't show on the surface.

Either leave the piece like this, or have the whole piece framed. There is a good argument for not using glass; I much prefer to be able to touch framed textiles, but you may want to protect your work from dust and dirty fingers.

Stitching on felt

Felt was my first fibre love affair. When I was eleven or twelve I used to catch a bus to Stockport, walk through narrow streets to the market, past the steamed-up cafés and pie shops, until I reached the glorious Victorian glass-covered indoor market. I wasn't interested in fruit and veg, cheap pegs and brushes, smashed biscuits and cinder toffee: all I wanted to look at were the fabric stalls.

There were two stalls at Stockport market that sold the 30cm (12in) felt squares I loved so much, in shades that have informed my colour sense ever since: lime green, shocking pink, deep purple, golden yellow, brilliant scarlet and hot, hot orange. I would hum and hah for ages, trying to decide which colours to buy, complicating the matter by deciding which sequins to buy as well.

And what did I do with my felt and sequins? Well, I had the best-dressed collection of trolls in Stockport, maybe in the whole north-west of England. Felt required so little sewing, never frayed and could be turned so quickly and easily into trolls' frocks, skirts, tops, towels, hats and scarves, and the glue-stuck sequins rarely fell off.

I have never lost my fondness for this soft and amazingly versatile fabric and was thrilled a few years ago to discover that as well as plenty of artisan, natural-dyed felts, there are now lots of fabulous felts in 100 per cent wool in all the deep and brilliant colours I like so much, sold in different-sized squares. Helpfully, some of these correspond to standard cushion pad sizes, so it turns out that felt is not only the fabric of choice for trolls, it is also perfect for making hand-stitched cushions. (And I've often thought that couture/dress designers should explore the possibility of troll-style zip-less, button-less felt collections.)

Felt features

Felt has many appealing qualities. It is lovely to touch, fantastically easy to cut, and makes a great sound when the scissors go through it. It is dense, springy and an ideal insulating fabric. It is soft, warm and flat but flexible. And, joy of joys, it doesn't fray. It is also a delight to stitch.

After years of using acrylic felt, I now prefer to use 100 per cent wool felt whose texture and properties I find preferable to wool/viscose, wool/acrylic, or 100 per cent acrylic felt. Wool felt is more expensive but it is wonderful to work with when stitching, and the needle glides through with a lovely smoothness. Wool is also beautifully matt and the colours that can be achieved are quite distinctive; pale colours are chalky and thick, and bright colours are brilliant and pure.

For most craft projects 1-mm ($^1/_{16}$-in) thick felt is what you need: 5mm ($^1/_4$in) felt is good for placemats, slippers, trivets and so on, but 1mm ($^1/_{16}$in) felt is widely available, very adaptable and thick enough to be good for many applications. Anything thinner than 1mm ($^1/_{16}$in) can be too flimsy and may come apart with wear.

Woven or knitted wool fabric that has been felted produces a quite different type of felt to that made by felting loose fibres. I use the felted-fibre felt, although felted woven or knitted fabric is a reasonable substitute for these projects as long as it has been well and truly felted and does not fray at the edges.

For where to buy felt, see Resources on page 158.

Hexagon Quilt

When I was planning this book, my conscience told me I should include a hexagon quilt. To my mind, the old-fashioned hexagon quilt is the ultimate in dainty, patient, painstaking stitching. It involves tacking hand-cut fabric hexagons over paper templates, then neatly stitching all the sides of the hexagons together with tiny stitches to make a top, plus quilting and finishing it all, preferably by hand. It seems to me that a single hexagon quilt could contain a whole lifetime's stitching. (I once hand-stitched a single small honeycomb piece with about twenty hexagons and that was quite enough.)

Nevertheless, I adore the look of hexagon/honeycomb quilts and the visual fun they can create. My favourites are the older, vintage quilts that include masses of different fabrics. The cleverest I have ever seen are those that were stitched entirely by hand by the novelist Lucy Boston — how she managed to hold the pattern in her head is quite amazing.

But having seen a couple of contemporary felt quilts/patchworks, it occurred to me that the way to make a super-simple hexagon quilt was to use felt. It would involve no backing templates, no folding over and no basting. I could simply cut out the hexagons, lay them out and stitch them on to a backing fabric. Perfect.

Felt is ideal for shapes that would otherwise be tricky and time-consuming to piece with traditional lightweight cottons. Felt blocks slot together brilliantly and most shapes with multiple angles — not just hexagons — work well, sitting nice and flat on the surface, making it the ideal medium for all those diamonds, parallelograms and rhombi that are far too daunting a prospect in other fabrics.

Design

I used a hexagon template to make this quilt (see page 151). From the internet I downloaded a sheet of various template sizes, which could be printed off. Initially, I wanted to make a reusable template to draw around and cut one out of quilter's template plastic, but this turned out to be slippery and very difficult to hold in place. So I simply printed off several sheets of my chosen hexagon template on paper, cut these out, pinned them to the felt, drew around them and cut out the fabric with the template still attached. Because this can sometimes lead to a little trimming of the paper shape, I used fresh templates whenever this happened. (Firm cardboard templates are an alternative, but they are difficult to pin on and can slip when you are drawing around them.)

Once I had sorted out template issue, I chose a group of colours I thought worked well together. Felt colours are so deep and rich and potentially overpowering that you have to choose carefully. I find that a limited palette in similar tones (depths of colour) works well, especially if you take a set of deep tones and a set of light tones.

I did think of creating the classic hexagon flower pattern with a central piece and six hexagons around it, or making a long diamond pattern, another popular way of using hexagons. But in the end, I simply cut out a dozen or so hexagons of each colour and started playing with them on the floor, lining them up and seeing what happened. Quite quickly I liked the look of stripes of alternating paler then deeper colours (of course, if you turn the piece through 90 degrees, you get a quite different effect). I was happy to leave it as simple as that; there is always so much going on in a hexagon quilt that the eye will find many more patterns in addition to the basic one.

Once I had sorted out my repeat pattern, I laid out all the hexagons, cutting out more as I went along, on the backing fabric. For the latter I used felt again, for several reasons. It sticks well to felt (think of Fuzzy Felt, the wonderful children's toy that, marvellously, you can still buy), it is very easy to stitch through two layers of felt, and because it doesn't fray, there is no edge-finishing and the excess can just be cut away like excess pastry on a pie crust. I used a wide piece of wool/viscose felt in a colour that was close to one of the shades in the top. Basic wool-mix felt can be bought in wide widths from fabric shops, but an old felted blanket or piece of wool backing made from felted jumpers would work and, if the back is likely to fray, the edges could be sewn over with blanket stitch (see page 148).

Once I was satisfied with the layout, I pinned on the hexagons and stitched them on to the backing felt with running stitch. Since the stitches will show on the reverse, you may prefer to stitch each hexagon individually, but as I am not a perfectionist I took the thread from hexagon to hexagon — and ended up liking the spidery effect on the back. So often we cover up the backs of work or are ashamed to show them, but these days there is a much greater openness about stitching, and a celebration of its very visibility: be proud of your stitches, show them off and let them be seen.

As for stitching thread, I tried a few different types before using two strands of cotton perlé 8. However, if I were to make another felt hexagon quilt, I would use cotton perlé 5 as it shows up beautifully and lies flat on the felt. If you don't have cotton perlé, it's worth trying different threads until you find something that works well with felt. (But I do know through trial and error that DMC/Anchor tapestry wools do not.)

To make the felt hexagon quilt

You will need

- Piece of felt or fabric measuring 90 x 30cm (35½ x 12in) (it will be trimmed to fit) for the backing (see details, right)
- You will need a quantity of 100 per cent wool felt for the top (see details, right)
- Sharp embroidery needle
- Thread for stitching (I recommend cotton perlé 5)
- Pins
- Soft pencil or air-erasable pen or chalk pencil to draw around templates
- 4cm (1½in) hexagon template (see page 151, or download sheets from the internet), photocopied on to paper or card and cut out

Finished size: approximately 75 x 50cm (30 x 20in).

Fabrics

Backing: this could be wool/viscose felt, or 100 per cent wool felt or an old felted blanket. If you want to make a different-sized quilt, the backing will determine the final size. Felt makes wonderful cosy, warm throws and quilts that can be practical and decorative, so think as large as you like and buy accordingly.

Top: you will need 104 hexagons. I used seven colours, but any combination is possible. The felt can come from a number of small felt squares that are then cut up and used completely, or from larger pieces, in which case you may have leftovers (depending on the size of the project). A 45cm (18in) square of felt will yield 25 hexagons (more if you can place them in perfect honeycomb formation before cutting). I tend to keep a selection of felt squares for cutting and come back to them time and time again. (See pages 60—69 for ideas for using up felt scraps.)

Making

Pin the template(s) to the felt. Draw around the template and cut out a number of hexagons in different colours. Play with the pieces, experimenting with different patterns, until you are happy with the layout; turn to page 63 for more thoughts on this. Cut more hexagons as you go until you are happy with the size and layout.

Pin each hexagon to the backing fabric. Stitch each hexagon in place on to the backing fabric with running stitch. When all the hexagons have been stitched on, trim the edges of the backing. If the raw edges are likely to fray and fraying is not something you want to happen, stitch them with blanket stitch (see page 148).

It really is as easy as that.

Tuppence Cushion

Even though I am now a lot older than twelve, felt squares still hold enormous appeal (I buy 45cm/18in squares). Their shape makes them the perfect grown-up Fuzzy Felt board on which felt shapes can be arranged and stitched, then quickly and easily turned into cushions. In fact, it's quite possible to make these Tuppence Cushions totally by hand, which is what I did. So if you don't have a sewing machine or the inclination to use one, these could be for you.

A while ago, for my yarnstorm blog, I knitted a series of cushions with rows of angora spots on plain wool backgrounds. I found much of my colour inspiration in a jar of jelly beans, so these became known as the Jelly Bean Cushions. But it seems I haven't exhausted my passion for spots and dots on cushions, and I found myself automatically coming up with a stitched variation for this book.

Felt creates such beautiful, clear cut-out shapes in brilliant colours that little dots seemed the obvious choice, although I did play with little squares (like a paintbox) but those didn't work as well as I'd hoped. I'm all for an easy life, even with stitching, and am not keen on special equipment when you can utilise what you already have, nor do I want to buy pre-cut felt shapes. So I looked around the house for a suitable circular template and found that a two-pence coin (2.5cm/1in in diameter) worked perfectly. (It also has a flat edge, not a ridged one, so the pencil doesn't bump up and down as it goes around it). However you could use any small coin of any currency; it doesn't have to be this diameter — a little smaller or larger would still be fine.

I had a few squares of 100 per cent wool felt in a range of high-summer foliage and flower colours, and decided to put shades of green on orange.

I wanted to make a second, reversed version but didn't have a full square of a bright green; with complete disregard for any forward planning, I had cut into all of them for the spots. But as I always like to begin a series rather than just make one of a kind, I did make a second green-on-orange cushion using different shades (some felt colours come in the most fantastic variety of shades).

The cushion needed something around the edge to finish it off; I like bobbles and fancy trimmings on cushions, but these can be horribly expensive. So I decided to make a felt trim, which is very easy as you only need strips to fit around the felt square.

I used my two-pence piece again as a template to make a scalloped edge across the 45cm (18in) width. Your template may or may not fit neatly a specific number of times across the felt, so cut a strip of paper and experiment beforehand with a pattern if necessary.

So this is the Tuppence Cushion, 'tuppence' being a much nicer way of saying 'two pence', as well as an old-fashioned term of endearment, especially for young children (maybe even what I was called by the market traders in Stockport all those years ago).

You will need

- ❖ Two squares of wool felt to fit a standard–sized cushion pad — my cushions are 45 x 45cm (18 x 18in), but any size square will work equally well and you can adjust the density of spots to suit the background
- ❖ Small amounts of contrasting colours (I had four different shades of green) to make the spots
- ❖ Spot and scallop templates on page 151, or circular template of your choice
- ❖ 15—20cm (6—8in) of felt the same width as the cushion front/back to make four 4—5cm (1½—2in) strips for the scalloped trimming
- ❖ Thread for stitching (I used cotton perlé 8 but any similar–thickness decorative thread would work)
- ❖ Cushion pad — mine is 45 x 45cm (18 x 18in)
- ❖ Fine pins
- ❖ Soft marker pen or pencil (any ordinary pencil will do, just make sure the marks are always on the underside or inside)

Making

Cut out the spots using your circular template of choice, or use the one on page 151. You can use any size of spot and number of spots you like. Mark the outline with a soft pencil or erasable pen/pencil whose marks can be brushed off later. I cut out seven lines of seven spots, so a total of 49 spots.

Lay out the spots the right way up (no pencil markings showing) on the background square. Mine are placed in vertical rows with three colours used twice. Hold each spot in place with a fine pin.

Sew each spot on with a star (see detail, opposite), always taking the needle from the outside edge down into the centre of the stitch so that you make a little depression in the centre.

You could make a back that is the reverse of the front (mine would be a variety of orange spots on a green background), or a different spotty colourway. Or you can leave the back plain.

Now make the scallop trim. Cut out four strips 4—5cm (1½—2in) wide to fit along the edges of the cushion front. Enlarge the scallop template on page 151 by 200 per cent. Pin the scallop to each strip, draw around it and cut it out. If you are using a different circular template for the spots, then make scallops to match. Along one edge of each strip, draw around the top half of your template, keeping the semicircles as close together as possible to make a scalloped edge.

Place the cushion top on the backing square, wrong sides facing, and line up the edges. Now place the four scallop trims along each side, slipping the straight edge between the front and the back so that the scalloped edges show, and pin the sides together. Make sure all the edges are lined up neatly and

that the cover lies flat before stitching.

Using your thread of choice (I used cotton perlé 8), hand–stitch three sides together about 5mm (¼in) in from the edges — stitching through the front, back and trim. Alteratively, stitch the edges on a sewing machine. Insert the cushion pad and sew up the fourth side.

Pin Money Pincushion

One of the many good things about felt is that you can use even the tiniest offcut or leftover in a stitching project. I found I had lots of little scraps that were just big enough for me to draw around a five-pence coin to make little circles to go on a pincushion. As this project is about pins and small change, I called it a Pin Money Pincushion, pin money traditionally being the small amounts of money earned by or given to women to spend on themselves for little luxuries such as pins.

So in the spirit of penny-pinching and household thrift, I used what I could find in the house for the templates. A saucer (free), 14cm (5½in) in diameter, was the template for the top and bottom. It doesn't have to be this size, and you could use any saucer or plate you like; with a big serving plate you could even make this into a large circular cushion and fill it with a cushion pad. A sixpence coin is the ideal size for the spots on a 14cm (5½in) top (if you make a bigger version, you will need to find a different template to make larger spots), but any small coin will do.

As with the Tuppence Cushion, I used four or five shades of a single colour for the spots — pink and orange/yellow — this time on a slate grey background. The pink version has thirteen spots, and the orange has fourteen spots, which just shows how much you play about with this sort of stitched project.

Once I had cut out the spots, the top and the bottom, it was simply a matter of pinning on the spots (just on the top circle) and stitching them on before sewing together the top and bottom like a cream-filled biscuit. I used blanket stitch in silver grey cotton perlé 8 on the pink version and slate grey cotton perlé 8 on the orange, left an opening and filled the cushion with polyester stuffing before completing the stitching.

Then all you have to do is buy some matching-colour glass-headed pins with the pin money you have saved from making your own pincushion. (It pleases me that it also ends up looking a little like a coin.)

You will need

❖ Enough felt to cut out two circles 14cm (5½in) in diameter
❖ Enough felt to cut out 13 or 14 little spots 1.75cm (¾in) in diameter
❖ Pincushion and spot templates on page 151, or a saucer/plate and coin the desired sizes
❖ Thread for stitching (I used cotton perlé 8 but any similar-thickness decorative thread would work)
❖ Stuffing (I used polyester, but any stuffing will do)
❖ Pins
❖ Soft marker pen or pencil (any ordinary pencil is fine — just be sure to keep the spots and the top and bottom the right way up so the lines don't show)

Making

Place template or the saucer (upside down) on the felt, draw around it and cut out two circles, one each for the top and bottom.

Drawing around a sixpence or similar, or the given template, cut out thirteen or fourteen little felt spots. Arrange the spots on the top circle to suit and pin them on.

Stitch each spot in place in the same way as for the Tuppence Cushion (see page 67), but using six, not eight, stitches.

Holding the top and bottom circles flat together, stitch around the outside using blanket stitch (see page 148). Leave a small opening, stuff until firm, then complete the stitching.

Stick in some pins.

Half-crazy patchwork

I am quite sure that true crazy patchwork divides people into two camps: those who love its craziness and mismatching madness of fabrics and stitches, and those who can't stand the busyness, the demands on the eye, the sheer overload of detail.

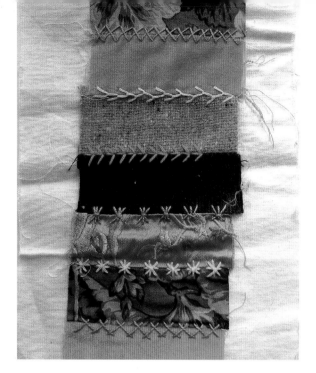

Fully crazy patchwork was immensely popular in the mid- to late nineteenth century, when it was the epitome of ladies' 'fancy work', made to sell at charity bazaars and to decorate already similarly over-decorated Victorian interiors. It combined rich fabrics, appliqué, embroidery, ribbons, sequins, charms, lace, beads and, seemingly, any embellishments the ladies could get their hands on. Some pieces were made wholly from random scraps, some — often collaborative projects — were made up of crazily pieced squares, and some combined random elements with more formal shapes such as fans or circles. After piecing and stitching, the makers often added more decoration and, in many cases, made it all too much. Despite this, and whatever your personal view of such richness and detail, these beautifully stitched items are still marvellous samplers of vintage textiles, and many must have had all sorts of memories of suits and shawls, dresses and hat ribbons sewn into them.

The craze for crazy patchwork died down in the twentieth century as quilters made more practical quilts that could be used and washed regularly. Nevertheless, in the first half of the twentieth century there was still some craziness in smaller items such as tea cosies and cushions that used up and showed off scraps of special and luxury fabrics. This was also the time when less ornate crazy patchworks were made with simpler, more everyday furnishing and dress fabrics. Today there is a renewal of interest in crazy patchwork, particularly in the USA, where it is almost a textile version of the highly popular scrapbooking in which all sorts of different elements are combined to create surface interest, and often to commemorate or celebrate events and people.

Fully crazy inspiration

Although I struggle to like the certifiably mad style, I still find myself drawn to traditional crazy patchwork. I like simplified versions which feature interesting fabrics that have been edited rather than added madly, and classic stitches that hold it all together such as feather and herringbone. In particular, I admire the crazy patchwork that shows a certain level of restraint and selection, as illustrated by the wonderful vintage tea cosy I found on eBay, a detail of which is shown opposite. This is a beautiful example of classic crazy patchwork rather than the over-the-top, bizarre bazaar style. Since I wanted to have a go at crazy patchwork myself, I analysed what it was that made this appealing.

Fabrics

These are mostly solid colours in silks and velvets (probably not all natural fibres), plus some very nice woven fabrics — including a few with stripes, which may have once been jacket linings. The fabrics have been chosen carefully and the maker has not simply thrown together everything that was at the bottom of her scraps bag.

Colours

A carefully selected and controlled mix of muted deep reds and blacks (the two classic crazy patchwork colours), lightened by various shades of sapphire, bronze, ochre, gold and ecru that are all of similar tones. As a result, they are not all competing and fighting with their neighbours.

Stitches

The whole tea cosy is embroidered mostly in one stitch — feather stitch — with a little bit of herringbone in places. The simplicity of one stitch works well in such a densely packed, small piece of patchwork, and it is worked in a very natural-looking, relaxed way that makes the stitch look different along different lines. So, the lesson here is that less is more.

Threads

These are all cotton perlé in very pale colours — peach, pink, baby blue and ivory — which keep the 'look' together and make the stitches stand out: after all, you want your carefully hand-worked stitching to show. This illustrates that cotton perlé is the ideal thread for this type of stitching (something generations of stitchers have known), and that it's best to gather together your threads before starting to make sure that they (a) work together and (b) will show off your work.

Only half-crazy design

True crazy patchwork is worked on a foundation or backing fabric such as muslin or calico. The fabric pieces are placed so that they overlap and they are then tacked on, usually with the visible raw edges turned under, but sometimes with the raw edges left as they are. The stitching and any other embellishments are then added, after which the patchwork is finished and made up. Some crazy patchwork quilts have a wadding, others don't — the finished top may be thick enough anyway. If there is a visible backing it is usually tied — rather than quilted — to the top, with the ends showing on the back as tufts or any further stitching would spoil the look of the top. This is why crazy patchwork is well suited to small items whose backs won't be seen, or that can be backed without the need for further quilting to hold layers together: for example cushion covers, tea cosies, bags, framed pictures, box covers and pincushions.

Although this technique seemed straightforward enough, I still didn't want all the crazy piecing and having to deal with hand-cut oddments, wacky scraps and weird angles. Instead, I wanted something with the spirit of crazy patchwork, but with much simpler shapes and faster cutting-out and stitching processes. By taking the elements and simplifying them, the results are less hectic and have a beauty in their rhythm and repetition, whereas truly crazy quilts can be maddening to the eye. So I took the idea of pieces of rich, gorgeous fabrics and fancy hand-stitched stitches in vivid colours, and applied them to rotary-cut, machine-pieced, completely regular shapes. I ended up with a half-crazy quilt that won't send you half crazy making it.

With each piece of half-crazy patchwork, my starting point was a deeply coloured patterned patchwork cotton with unusual shades and colour combinations. I then picked out various colours in luxurious fabrics such as velvet, silk, tweed and corduroy. Some of these were from discarded clothing and some were bought specially; a half-crazy quilt is as good a reason as any to cut up old jackets, skirts, evening and bridesmaid's dresses that will otherwise never again see the light of day. Alternatively, as the amount needed of any one fabric is very small, you can splash out on a small length of cotton velvet, silk, tweed, ticking, corduroy or satin without it hurting too much, and some fabric shops have a minimum cut as small as 10cm (4in), which is ideal.

Stitches that won't drive you crazy

Crazy patchwork can be as mad and multicoloured or as sane and simple as you like. It can be an opportunity to try out every decorative stitch in the book — or to invent your own pretty scheme using combinations of various classic stitches — and to use every colour and thread that takes your fancy. Or it can be more controlled and feature just a few favourite stitches in a small range of colours using one type of thread. Or you can even go minimalist (which sounds like a contradiction in terms in the context of crazy patchwork, but isn't), by employing a single type of stitch and a single colour on a simple combination of fabrics.

I found it very useful to practise a mix of old favourites and new discoveries on a small experimental piece of half-crazy patchwork. I also used this as an opportunity to try out different threads in different colours (cotton perlé 5, cotton perlé 8 used double, six-strand cotton embroidery thread and silk threads in different thicknesses) and was very sure as a result that I preferred cotton perlé 5 in clearly visible colours for this type of stitching. This little sampler proved to be a useful reference when it came to making the full pieces.

Two classic stitches

I always think of herringbone and feather stitch (see pages 144 and 146) as the classic crazy patchwork stitches; they are the ones that always appear on old pieces of crazy patchwork and look good every time. The appearance of both stitches can be altered by varying the length, width and placement, so they are very useful stitches indeed to have in your repertoire.

Two pretty stitches

Although sheaf stitch (see page 147) and star stitch take time to complete and use up a large amount of thread, they are worth working simply because they look beautiful, and add glamour and interest to any crazy patchwork project. (Star stitch is simply two cross stitches — see page 145 — worked at different angles on top of each other.)

Two fancy stitches

More elaborate-looking stitches don't have to be ones that are difficult to work. Cretan stitch and wheat-ear stitch (see pages 147 and 149) are suitably intricate to the eye, but easier on the fingers than they look.

Half-Crazy Cushion

After a little practice, I moved on to a larger version of the experimental piece with slighter bigger rectangles. This sampler — which became a cushion cover but could have been used in many different ways, or simply framed — began with a leftover length of a geranium print by Philip Jacobs with an unusual colour combination of teal, bright pink, purple and old gold. It seemed a good place to start, having something in common with deep and dark Victorian aesthetics, but also having a contemporary feel.

I carried this 'lead fabric' around with me, looking for complementary fabrics, and found an old pair of cord trousers and a skirt that picked out some of the colours, plus some small pieces of silk left over from another quilt. I bought a couple of 25cm (10in) lengths of new cotton velvet to add richness and depth and added in a tweed, a shocking pink very fine needlecord, a Kaffe Fassett 'Aboriginal Dots' cotton fabric and a Japanese floral fabric with big, swirling stylised flowers. I found the key to keeping it all relatively calm — rather than mad — was to stick closely to the colours in the lead fabric and to keep the number of fabrics used relatively small.

I had already decided that rectangles rather than squares or any other shape would work best and also be easy to handle. Rectangles allow the lines of stitching to be close together, as they are in fully crazy patchwork, and present nice, straight seams along which to stitch. I experimented with different sizes and settled on cutting out 5 x 9cm (2 x 3½in for those with an inch-marked quilter's rule) rectangles to make 4 x 8cm (1½ x 3in) rectangles, although I must stress that the shape and size of the pieces in half-crazy patchwork can be varied to suit what's available, how much stitching time one has and what

the finished article is to be. I say that now, but when I started this, I had no idea what it would be. A cushion cover was just a vague possibility, which is why the finished article is not the exact size of a standard cushion pad, but is close enough to work. I backed my cushion with a piece of hot-pink velvet extended with a strip of shocking-pink needlecord, as I didn't have quite enough velvet.

To make the cushion

You will need

- ❖ A total of 50cm (20in) of 106-cm (42-in) wide fabrics (see below)
- ❖ Rotary cutter, ruler and cutting mat
- ❖ Sewing machine
- ❖ Neutral-coloured sewing thread
- ❖ Iron
- ❖ Pins
- ❖ Foundation fabric (see details below), measuring 10—15cm (4—6in) larger than the proposed patchwork
- ❖ A selection of threads, such as cotton perlé 8 (see page 72), for fancy stitching
- ❖ Embroidery needle
- ❖ Backing fabric measuring 62 x 62cm (24½ x 24½in)
- ❖ 60cm x 60cm (23¾ x 23¾in) cushion pad
- ❖ Sewing needle

Finished size: 60 x 60cm (23¾ x 23¾in). Note: you can enlarge the project and use any shape and size of shape to make a half-crazy quilt top. Adjust your fabric requirements accordingly, and use the same basic making process as given for the cushion. Take 5mm (¼in) seam allowances throughout.

Fabrics

The patchwork fabrics should comprise a lead fabric, if you choose to select one to act as a colour catalyst, plus assorted small pieces or short lengths of fabrics that work together and/or with the lead fabric. Use fabrics such as cord, velvet, cotton, wool, tweed and silk.

The foundation fabric can be medium-weight calico, cotton sheeting or an old pillowcase.

Making

You will need a total of 105 rectangles, each measuring 5 x 9cm (2 x 3½in), in a variety of fabrics. I prefer to cut out a few rectangles at a time and cut out more as I go along, once I can see which fabrics are working well together.

Lay out the rectangles and move them around until you are happy with the arrangement. Machine-sew rectangles together in strips. Press open the seam allowances, taking care with any delicate fabrics. Then sew the strips together to make the whole patchwork cushion top. Press open the second lot of seam allowances.

Pin the finished top to the piece of foundation fabric. Stitch the vertical seams with your choice of embroidery stitches (see page 74). You can also stitch the horizontal seams if you want.

Trim the foundation fabric to match the patchwork and measure the piece. If need be, cut down the backing fabric so that it is the same size as the patchwork. Pin the pieces right sides together. Leaving the seam that will be at the bottom of the cushion open, machine-sew around the other three sides, taking a 1cm (³⁄₈in) seam allowance. Turn the cover right side out and insert the cushion pad. Pin the remaining seam and neatly hand-stitch it closed. If you prefer, insert a zip to close the cover.

Milly Tea Cosy

One of my favourite children's book characters is Milly–Molly–Mandy in the stories by Joyce Lankester Brisley. Milly–Molly–Mandy is a delightful little girl, who enjoys all sorts of simple, old–fashioned, village and domestic adventures and is always willing to try something new. In a lovely story called 'Milly–Molly–Mandy Makes a Cosy', she is inspired by Miss Muggins' beautiful tea cosy made of bright silks and velvets finished off with cord. She secretly collects scraps of red satin, green ribbon, black velvet, lavender ribbon, cord and blue and yellow spotty tie fabric, asks Aunty to teach her how to do feather stitch, and produces a beautiful handmade cosy to surprise her mother.

Rereading the story, I saw it as a challenge. If a little girl could make a crazy patchwork cosy, then surely I could make a half–crazy patchwork cosy? The Milly Tea Cosy is the result (not Milly–Molly–Mandy, as I have taken shortcuts with the making).

This is a very simplified version of crazy patchwork cosies and uses just herringbone stitch in a single colour of thread, but could be made much fancier with a range of different stitches (see page 74) in different colours. The cosy uses a simple strippy quilt base that is cut into two, then each piece is cut into a cosy shape, stitched, then sewn back together.

Many vintage crazy tea cosies are padded, but some have an inner pad that can be removed. I opted for the latter as it makes the process simpler. I used a double thickness of felt cut to fit inside the finished cover, machine–sewed the edges and simply slipped it inside the cover.

To make the tea cosy

You will need

- Ten strips of fabric (see details, right), each measuring 75 x 5cm (29½ x 2in) (you can join a few shorter strips to make the length if necessary)
- Sewing machine
- Neutral-coloured cotton sewing thread
- Iron
- Pins
- Twp pieces of foundation fabric (see details, right), each measuring approximately 45 x 45cm (18 x 18in)
- Tea cosy template (see page 152)
- Fading fabric marker
- A selection of threads, such as cotton perlé 8 (see page 74), for fancy stitching
- Embroidery needle
- Four pieces of felt, each measuring 40 x 30cm (15¾ x 12in)
- Sewing needle
- Cord to finish (optional)

Finished size: approximately 27cm (10½in) deep by 38cm (15in) across at largest points.

Fabrics

When selecting patchwork fabrics I find it helps to choose a 'lead' fabric, then select a few silks, velvets and cotton prints and velvets to go with it. Alternatively, just use up desirable scraps of rich fabrics with some sort of colour guiding principle.

The foundation fabric can be medium-weight calico, cotton sheeting or an old pillowcase.

Making

Pin two strips right sides together and, taking a 5mm (¼in) seam allowance, machine-sew one seam. Pin another strip to one raw edge and machine-sew that seam, starting from the end the previous seam finished at. Repeat to sew all the strips together, alternating the starting end of the seams to help prevent the patchwork distorting.

Press the seams either open or to one side to make the piece as flat as possible (not all fabrics will lie well in the same direction).

Cut the piece horizontally into two halves, each measuring approximately 37 x 37cm (14½ x 14½in). Pin each half on to a piece of foundation fabric.

Enlarge the template by 200 per cent and pin it to the right side of one patchwork piece, aligning the edges of the template with the edges of the patchwork. Draw around it with the fabric marker. Alternatively, measure out and mark the centre point of the arc and draw the shape freehand on the fabric. Cut the other patchwork piece to match the first one.

Stitch along the seams using whichever stitch(es) you like — I used just herringbone stitch in only one colour of thread.

Trim the foundation fabric to match the patchwork. Pin the pieces right sides together and, taking a 5mm (¼in) seam

allowance, machine-sew up the sides and around the curve, leaving the bottom open. Turn right side out and press. Zigzag stitch around the bottom edge to neaten it, then turn up the bottom edge by 2.5cm (1in) and hand-sew the hem.

Make the felt inner pad by cutting out one piece using the tea cosy template. Trim it so that it fits inside the cosy, then use it as a template to cut three more pieces. Pin all four pieces together and machine-sew up the sides and around the curve, leaving the bottom open. Push the pad inside the cosy, opening it up so that there are two layers of fabric on either side of the teapot.

Finish by hand-sewing a length of cord along the seam of the tea cosy (cord can also be added along the two lower edges if you want), making a small loop at the top centre for lifting the cosy.

Suffolk puffs

Suffolk puffs (also known in the US as fabric yo-yos or pom-poms) have to be one of the most effective and attractive uses of basic running stitch. It's the ultimate in happy hand-stitching, and there are all sorts of clever things and effects you can create with a pile of puffs.

A Suffolk puff is a circle of fabric which is transformed into a beautiful, evenly gathered rosette of fabric simply by making a line of running stitch around the outside, folding the edge over as you go, pulling up the thread once you have come back to the start point, then finishing off.

Despite their grandly historical name (I imagine medieval ladies sitting in wide window seats in draughty, moated Suffolk houses making little puffs from silk brocade), there is very little in the way of written information about them. They were popular in the first half of the twentieth century, and the fact that many lovely Suffolk puff quilts and yo-yo quilts were being made at the same time in Britain, North America, Australia and New Zealand suggests that many stitchers have known for many years that Suffolk puffs are an excellent and decorative way to use up scraps of fabric.

Fabrics

Puffs and yo-yos do funny things with fabric patterns and I think it is worth taking this into account when choosing fabrics. They change the look of a fabric dramatically; it's quite magical watching the fabric alter as you pull a flat, circular piece, on which a design and repeat is clear, into a textured circle with a randomly altered pattern.

Some fabrics that don't look terribly exciting work beautifully and create a lovely surprise, while others that you think are sure to look good lose something in the process and look less than they originally were. The latter includes abstract designs and anything hazy and blurred, which can lose even more definition in the pulling-in, whereas anything that is very definite works extremely well: spots, stripes and small-scale checks look wonderful as puffs. I also find that puffs work brilliantly with small-detail prints such as those on reproduction nineteenth-century quilting fabrics (for example, Civil War designs), and with 1930s/ditsy Aunt Grace fabrics. There is great pleasure to be had in working closely with delightful details and subtle colours that are so small that you can miss them when working on a larger scale or on a machine.

Any lightweight cotton is ideal; in the past, feedsack, shirting and dress cottons were used to make beautiful Suffolk puff quilts, cushion covers, tea cosies and table mats. These days, quilting fabrics are perfect, as are dressmaking cottons, ginghams, and recycled dresses, skirts and shirts. Satins and silks (such as dupion or shot silk) look good but are much more slippery and difficult to handle than cotton, which doesn't move when you fold over and hold down the edge while sewing. You may need to use small pins with

silky fabrics, and for me the whole point of this sort of simple stitching is that you can make lots of puffs in very little time (I average around fifteen to sixteen puffs during the length of a film). Other fabrics such as wools and tweeds and brushed cottons do work, but remember that the thicker the fabric, the thicker the folded edge and the harder it is to close the centre and produce a relatively neat and unbulky rosette.

When it comes to colours, it pays to keep to a carefully chosen palette as the density of the ruffled fabric is pretty intense on the eye anyway, and although a random, pick 'n' mix sweetshop selection might look tempting when cut out as circles, it can soon turn very busy when turned into puffs. Some reproduction prints with tiny motifs create beautiful puffs when viewed close up, but their small details tend to make the colours blur when seen from a distance and they can appear sludgy, so it's best to break up the layout with some spots or stripes.

If you want something that makes an impact when you walk into a room, base your selection on two bright, fresh colours that go well together (see the pink and yellow quilt on page 88), or use a deep colour to contrast with one or two light colours. It's best to avoid very large prints that look great as cut-out circles but very indifferent and undistinguished as puffs unless they have a very definite pattern that is not destroyed by ruching.

Needle and thread

Any standard sharps or slim embroidery needles will work: the kind of needle that is available everywhere and found at the bottom of workbaskets and sewing boxes. A relatively fine one is best as a thick needle is difficult to pull through the gathers of the fabric.

Ordinary cotton sewing thread is best. I recommend 100 per cent cotton for strength and longevity. Use the thread doubled to allow you to pull tightly without fear of snapping.

The maths

Suffolk puffs have always been made with scraps and offcuts and leftovers, and quilts probably grew organically as fabric became available. I doubt they were ever carefully calculated, and when I started making them, I followed suit.

First of all I had no idea how big a puff should be, so experimented with different household implements as my template. A compact disc made a puff 5.5cm (2¼in) in diameter, which was too small for my liking (I wanted something that would grow quite quickly), and a 14cm (5½in) saucer made a puff 7cm (2¾in) in diameter, which was almost right. Then, like Goldilocks, I tried a third template, a 16cm (6¼in) plate that produced the ideal 7.5cm (3in) puff, which is what you see in these photos.

You can make your puffs any size you like, from small to large, and the general rule of thumb is that the puff will be half the diameter of the original circle, although I find it is marginally smaller than that. This could be because my folding over at the edge might be a little more generous than other people's, although the fabric can be folded over by anything from 4—8mm (¼—½in) and there is no 'correct' fold–over measurement — just use what feels right to you. However, do bear in mind that it's important to be consistent so that all the puffs are more or less the same size (if that's what you want them to be).

If you do want to calculate your fabric requirements, you will find that puffs are very fabric–hungry and use up a surprisingly large amount. I can get 36 of my 7.5cm (3in) puffs (final measurement) out of 1m (39in) of 106-cm (42-in) wide quilting fabric, which gives a finished piece of sewn–together puffs measuring about 45 x 45cm (18 x 18in); six puffs across and six down.

How to make Suffolk puffs

It pays to iron the fabric before starting as it's not easy to iron finished puffs without squashing them. I don't cut out all my circles in advance, as I wait to see how each fabric design works as a puff before deciding which fabrics to use. Once I know, I cut out a few of each at a time as I go along.

Use a sturdy circular object (compact disc, saucer, small plate, jam jar lid) as a template and simply draw around it on the wrong side of the fabric with a pencil, pen, quilter's pen, or whatever you have to hand (best to choose something that doesn't go through to the right side, but even then it's not the end of the world as it won't show) and cut out the marked circle.

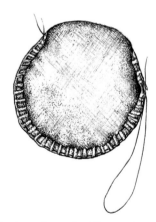

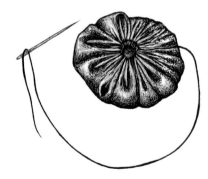

Thread a thinnish needle with everyday cotton and double it. You can make a knot if you like, but as the first stitch needs to be sewn over to anchor it firmly, this is not necessary.

With your non-needle-holding hand, fold over the edge of the fabric 4—8mm ($^1/_4$—$^1/_2$in) — but no more — and make the first stitch close to the edge. Sew over it several times, take the needle to the right side and work a line of running stitch close to the edge of the circle, folding the fabric over as you go; bear in mind that large stitches will give a smaller opening and small stitches will make a larger opening: I use quite small stitches.

When you have gone all around the edge, make sure you take the needle to the right side before pulling up the thread firmly to create a rosette-like puff. Now finish off by gently pulling out the puff so it lies flat, centring the hole in the middle and sewing over the last stitch several times (I am quite happy for my stitches to show, but you may want to make the stitches inside the puff).

Designs for puff quilts

As well as liking the old-fashioned, frilly-knicker appearance of Suffolk puffs, I find it hard to resist making anything with a whimsical name that sounds very much like the sort of nice jammy, creamy treat that you might find served for afternoon tea in the countryside. And this is why I have called my pink and yellow quilt the Jam and Custard Puff Quilt: the pinks make me think of fresh raspberry and cherry jam and the yellows of rich cream or custard that might be used to fill little puffy baked treats. So once I'd started with just a few fabrics and had my jam and custard theme, it was easy to add new fabrics to the mix.

The Historical Puffs Piece was also straightforward to plan, as I wanted to use up some reproduction nineteenth-century patchwork fabrics that feature very small, exquisite details and are characterised by their quite plain and earthy colours, colours I find quite dull in large-scale pieces within bigger quilts. Again, once I had the colour scheme (browns, deep reds, ochre, leaf greens, deep blues), it was very easy to select fabrics for inclusion.

Ways to use Suffolk puffs

❖ The obvious first-time project is a simple Suffolk puff quilt without any backing, stuffing, buttons or adornment because this, I think, is what Suffolk puffs are all about. It is the fastest, simplest, purest way of using them, and the interest comes partly from the background, which changes depending on where you place the quilt.

❖ Or you can sew the puffs on to a backing fabric to make a more solid quilt, throw, table mat or covering, cushion cover or bag.

❖ Use a row of puffs as a trim around the edge of a blanket or quilt, or on the bottom of a curtain or blind.

❖ Use individual puffs to decorate plain quilts or blankets, or as fabric brooches, or as a topper on a wrapped gift.

Making up a quilt

Suffolk puffs are an uncomplicated and gently satisfying way to enjoy hand-stitching in small, manageable, puff-size bites, and a traditional Suffolk puff quilt is much, much easier to make than other types of traditional hand-stitched quilts, such as hexagon quilts in which every piece has to be tacked over a paper template, then carefully sewn into place. For a start, there is far less anxiety about the basic template; with hexagons you have to be very accurate when cutting out to ensure that each side and angle interlocks perfectly with its neighbours, but Suffolk puffs can be made quickly and simply. Once you have stitched and pulled (no tacking involved), that's your puff done, which makes you feel very productive very quickly. And if the cutting-out is a little wobbly or the stitching less than perfect, no one will ever know because none of it shows in the finished puff.

Puffs can be made over time on an ad hoc basis and stored until you have enough to make a quilt or project. Alternatively, you can plan your puffs carefully by selecting a set number of fabrics and colours and working to a pre-planned layout. Puffs can be used in exactly the same way as other quilt pieces and built up into blocks, repeats and patterns. They can be set out randomly, in patterns, criss-crosses, rows, or however you like.

Once the layout has been decided, the puffs can be sewn together. Again, this is all done by hand and is incredibly easy. A few stitches at each of the north, south, east, west compass points is all that is needed. These can be done in a contrasting colour using two strands of embroidery thread or the same sewing thread used to make the puffs (which is what I do). Again, use doubled thread as it is much stronger.

The link between puffs can be just a few stitches or a couple of centimetres, depending on how dense and pulled together you want the quilt to be. I do simple overstitching, holding the 'wrong' sides (the flat backs) together and working about 1—1.5cm ($^3/_8$—$^5/_8$in) of stitching, making sure I sew over the beginning and end firmly. I have seen puffs that have been sewn together with minimal stitching, which makes a very open, loose quilt, and I have seen puffs that have been almost entirely sewn together which makes a very dense, closed quilt — and again like Goldilocks, I prefer something in between the two.

A Suffolk puff quilt is actually much sturdier than I imagined; I thought it would feel very delicate and be easily damaged, but in fact it is quite strong and heavy (all that gathered fabric makes it quite weighty), and a huge quilt would make a lovely topping for a bed or favourite chair. It is also possible to sew the puffs directly on to a backing fabric with small stitches to make a quilt top or cushion cover, but I much prefer to see Suffolk puffs as they are, with the gaps between them that change colour depending on the surface underneath. I also like seeing the reverse side, with all the little circles of flat fabric making such a contrast to the rosette side. Plus, there is enough hand-stitching in the making of the puffs themselves to keep me satisfied and busy, without making any more work for myself.

To make the Jam and Custard Quilt

Fabric requirements are based on a quilt using 7.5cm (3in) puffs with seventeen puffs across and seventeen puffs down (total of 289 puffs), but it's possible to make a quilt with any number of puffs, increasing or decreasing fabric quantities accordingly.

You will need
- ❖ A total of 10m (11yd) of 106-cm (42-in) wide lightweight cotton fabric (patchwork fabric, or old dresses, shirts, sheets and pillowcases, see details below)
- ❖ 100 per cent cotton sewing thread
- ❖ A fine, everyday sewing needle
- ❖ Plate 16cm (6¼in) in diameter (mine was a side plate) for the template OR use a template that suits you and make sure you adjust fabric quantities accordingly
- ❖ A fabric marker pen or soft pencil

Fabrics
I used a selection of pink and yellow fabrics, including fabrics from Denyse Schmidt's 'Flea Market Fancy' collection, Yuwa's 'Honeycomb', two colourways of Kaffe Fassett's 'Lotus Leaf', Amy Butler's 'Lotus Spot', and Philip Jacobs' 'Painted Daisies' and 'Waltzing Matilda'.

Making
Decide whether you are going to lay the puffs out in a pattern or in rows or in a random arrangement. This will help you plan the cutting-out and stitching. I just started making puffs and then added in fabrics I thought would work well, but didn't count the numbers of puffs per fabric, something that would be necessary if working in set rows or patterns.

Cut out and make the individual puffs, following the instructions on page 84.

Lay out the puffs and stitch them together as explained on page 86.

To make the Historical Puffs Piece

Fabric requirements are based on a piece using 7.5cm (3in) puffs with ten puffs across and ten puffs down (total of 100 puffs).

You will need
- ❖ A total of 3.5m (4yd) of 106-cm (42-in) wide lightweight cotton fabric (patchwork fabric, or old dresses, shirts, sheets and pillowcases, see details below)
- ❖ 100 per cent cotton sewing thread
- ❖ A fine everyday sewing needle
- ❖ Plate 16cm (6¼in) in diameter (mine was a side plate) for the template OR use a template that suits you and make sure you adjust fabric quantities accordingly
- ❖ A fabric marker pen or soft pencil

Fabrics
I used a selection of reproduction and tiny-motif fabrics by a range of designers and manufacturers. My favourite producer of traditional and reproduction designs is Windham Fabrics (www.windhamfabrics.com) and I just wish I could find more of them in the UK (they are more widely available in the US and on websites), although Fabric Inspirations (www.fabricinspirations.co.uk) has a decent selection. My fabrics include Moda Victoria's 'Crown Princess Feathers 1830–1865', 'New England Quilts' from Old Sturbridge Village's curator, Aimee Newell, Virginia Robertson for Fabri-Quilt, a couple of Denyse Schmidt's 'Flea Market Fancy' fabrics, Yuwa's 'Tea Cups' from the 'Live Life' collection, Windham's 'Eagle Medallion Collection', 'Echoes of the Past: Austen Manor' by Harriet Hargrave for P&B Textiles, 'Jo's Calicos' by Jo Morton for Andover Fabrics, Judie Rothermel's 'Old Sturbridge Village Collection' for Marcus Fabrics, 'Rocky Mountain Quilt Collection' by Judie Rothermel, Moda's 'Conestoga Calico Prairie Rose 1830–1860'.

Making
Follow the instructions for the Jam and Custard Quilt. For a photograph of the finished Historical Puffs Piece, see page 87.

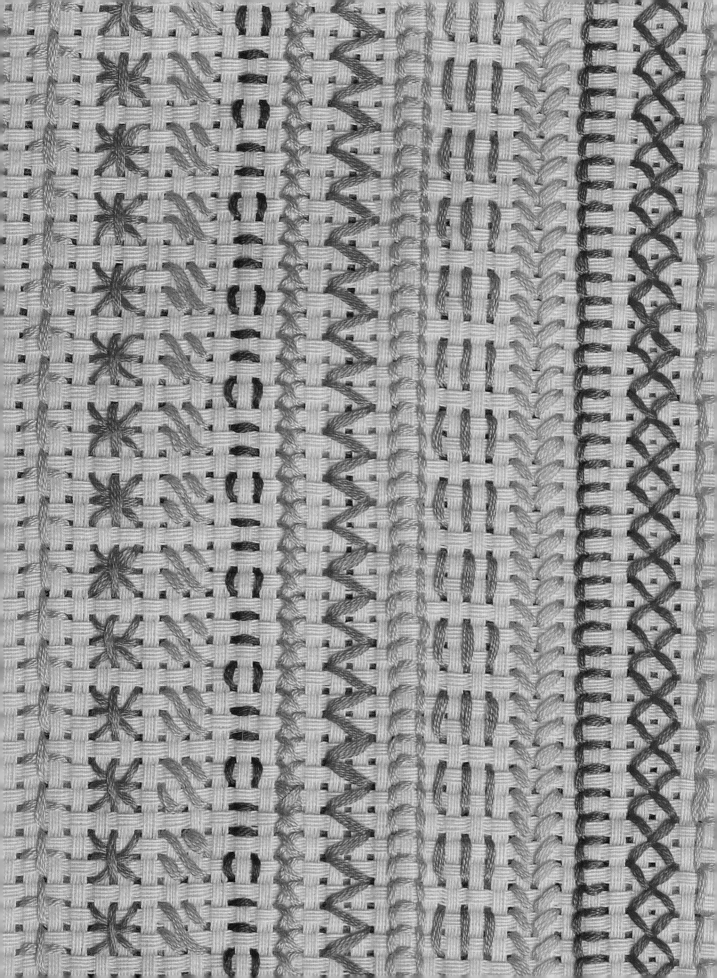

Lessons
in stitching

Binka canvas is the stuff of primary school — blunt needles, and lots of tongues sticking out as children concentrate on threading needles and making stitches. For me, it brings back vivid memories of Miss Beales' class, with 40 eight-year olds stitching — usually in winter or early spring when it was cold outside — to make Christmas and Mother's Day presents to take home.

The concentration in those schoolroom sewing sessions was such that the atmosphere usually became very hot and tense. Each one of us was given a piece of cream-coloured binka canvas, a chunky blunt needle and the choice of just three colours of thick cotton thread: red, blue and green. Then we sat and stitched, simply working in ever-decreasing rectangles of cross stitch, half-cross stitch and any stitch we could invent. I found that filling up the holes and covering the canvas was very satisfying (although I am quite sure many of my classmates hated this hour in the week with a passion), and rather like a massive dot-to-dot creation with colour, pattern and repetition. We made mats for our mums, and I enjoyed seeing my finished pieces on my mum's dressing table so much that I even started stitching binka canvas at home. No doubt I would have covered every surface in the house if another crafting hobby — felt and sequins (see page 60) — hadn't come along.

It now amazes me that while we were struggling with thick wool and large holes, a hundred years previously young girls of the same age were stitching beautiful samplers with fine threads on closely woven fabrics. I know that most stitchers move on to acquire similarly wonderful skills, but I have never completely deserted binka with its sheer manageability and the pleasure of large-scale stitches. Plus, it's the ideal way to get young stitchers enthused and involved (no marking-out, no rules, no frames, no sharp needles and no tears); they can use knots and big needles and doodle on the canvas and make it all up as they go along.

These days I still enjoy experimenting with the three different ways of joining up holes — vertically, horizontally and diagonally — but now I use six-strand embroidery thread or tapestry wool in as many colours as I like. And binka has its educational merits: it's possible to use it for stitching lessons if you follow a stitch directory written for cross stitch, sampler and needlepoint work. In this way you can practise and learn proper, traditional stitches with proper, traditional names — or you can simply have fun on your own and

make up stitches as you go along. Go big or small, simple or complex, be as colourful or as monochrome as you like, but most of all enjoy yourself with a needle and thread. These may be illiterate samplers by Victorian standards, but you might just create your own personal stitching grammar.

Binka canvas

The joy of binka canvas (6-count canvas, that is to say it has six holes per inch) is that it is so easy to work with. It has big holes and clear lines and self-evident grids, which mean it's very simple to keep everything straight and neat. It doesn't pull out of shape too much as it's quite pliable and soft, and is sturdy enough to hold in the hand and work on without a frame or hoop. The only minor downside is that it frays easily, so it's best to leave a wide border or to cover the raw edges with masking tape to hold the strands in place.

Binka also comes in several colours (I like the white and the ivory) and it is widely available in craft and hobby shops, department stores, haberdasheries and on websites. I prefer the binka made by Zweigart, although the manufacturer's name is not always clear.

Designs

On page 153 you will find charts for three different ways of exploiting the possibilities of binka canvas. There's a non-traditional, playful sampler worked in six-strand embroidery thread showing various stitches, many of which were made up as I stitched. This makes a nice piece for framing.

Then there's a chart for a stitched Valentine's heart that uses some of the same stitches and is worked in various shades of burgundy and dusty pink. The heart can be used on cards or gift tags, or you can frame it.

The final piece could be used as a mat, or it could be extended to make a larger item (such as a table runner), or it could be made into a little case for holding crochet hooks or suchlike, as has been done here.

To make the Playtime Sampler

You will need

- ❖ Binka/6-count canvas measuring approximately 30 x 40cm (12 x 16in)
- ❖ Masking tape
- ❖ Large, blunt tapestry needle
- ❖ Selection of six-strand cotton embroidery threads in the colours of your choice
- ❖ Chart (see page 153), or a stitch directory and/or imagination
- ❖ A pair of sharp scissors

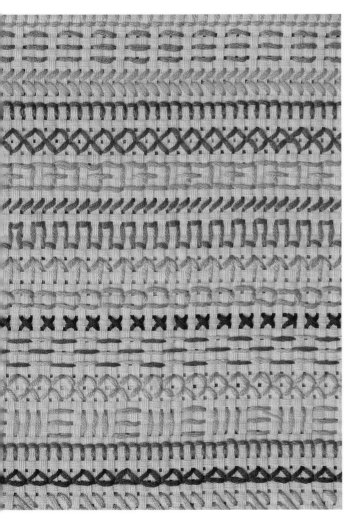

Making

Decide on the shape and size of the piece you are going to stitch (squares and rectangles make good samplers and mats). Allow an excess of at least 5cm (2in) around the outside of the stitching so that the piece can be framed or the fabric artfully frayed after completion. Fold a strip of masking tape over each edge to prevent fraying while stitching.

Thread a needle with stranded embroidery thread (use all six strands) and start stitching. If teaching a child, I would suggest making a knot to anchor the thread until he/she is able to start off by overstitching a couple of times. Or start by holding a tail of thread behind the first few stitches and sewing over it to hold it down.

You can follow the chart provided or make up your own patterns. Work in lines, sections, ever-decreasing squares or rectangles, or small sections to create a patchwork effect. Patterns can be stitched into shapes such as circles (to make 'baubles' for Christmas cards), hearts (to make Valentine's Day cards) or cakes (for birthday cards).

To finish, remove the masking tape and trim the edges/border to the desired finished size. If you are making a mat, you might want to fray the edges.

If you are framing a sampler, stitch the sampler to a piece of backing card. To do this, position the sampler on the card and, with a sharp needle, make two little holes at each corner and at points along the top, bottom and sides. Then, with a smaller needle and strong cotton thread in a colour to match the fabric, make a little stitch at each point to hold the sampler firmly in position, taking the thread from point to point on the back and finishing off securely. The piece can be left mounted simply and displayed, or it can be framed and held under glass.

If you are backing the sampler to make it more durable, you need a piece of fabric a couple of centimetres larger than the embroidery. Cotton fabric such as medium-weight calico, sheeting or patchwork cotton is fine. Or, if you are using the stitched binka as a mat, you could back it with felt. Place the fabrics right sides together and machine-sew around three sides, following the straight lines of the outside edge of the canvas. Trim if necessary. Turn the right way, and finish by turning in and neatly hand-sewing the fourth edge.

To make the Sweetheart Sampler

This tiny sampler takes an equally tiny amount of time to stitch.

You will need

- ❖ Binka/6-count canvas measuring approximately 14 x 14cm (5½ x 5½in)
- ❖ Masking tape
- ❖ Large, blunt tapestry needle
- ❖ Selection of six-strand cotton embroidery threads in shades of pink, maroon and deep red (or any colours you like)
- ❖ Heart chart (see page 153)
- ❖ A stitch directory and/or imagination
- ❖ A pair of sharp scissors

Making

Thread a needle with stranded embroidery thread (use all six strands), and follow the chart, or create your own stitches within the outline shape.

If you are making greetings cards, stitch the finished binka piece on to a pre-cut card in the same way as for a sampler (see page 93). You can use a 'window' or 'aperture' card, which folds up to allow the stitching to show through a pre-cut opening on the front of the card.

To make the Zigzag Case

This little project uses tapestry wool instead of embroidery cotton, and came about because I wanted to see what it was like to stitch with wool on binka again after all these years. Inspired by the colours of conkers and horse chestnut trees, I used leftover threads and stitched an all-over design using just diagonals (although you could use all cross stitches for this) in a pattern of rectangles. It's very simple and therapeutic, and a nice way to use up lengths of wool — the rectangles (a pattern with squares would work equally well) look like a mini patchwork quilt. I used various shades seen on conker trees: lime green for the new leaves, off-white for the flowers, darker greens for older leaves and deep brown for the conkers.

Not needing a mat, I decided to turn the embroidery into a little case that could hold the crochet hooks that have been spread out in drawers for far too long.

You will need

- ❖ Binka/6-count canvas measuring approximately 35 x 30cm (14 x 12in)
- ❖ Masking tape
- ❖ Large, blunt tapestry needle
- ❖ Selection of tapestry wools
- ❖ Zigzag rectangle chart (see page 153)
- ❖ A piece of backing fabric 2cm (³/₄in) larger all around than the stitched piece
- ❖ Button
- ❖ A pair of sharp scissors

Finished size: 20 x 10cm (8 x 4in).

Making

In your chosen colours, follow the chart for stitching a square and repeat it to fill the canvas. Or make up your own pattern of squares or rectangles using the half-cross zigzag stitch or cross stitch.

When you have finished the stitching, back the embroidery with a piece of fabric as for a sampler (see page 93).

Fold into three to make a case, placing the hand-sewn edge under the flap. Holding the side seams together on the right side, hand-sew in place with small overstitches.

Finish with a button and a loop of ribbon or plaited tapestry wools to close.

Alternatively, simply stitch any size of rectangle that, when folded over, will make a case the desired size. Back with fabric and finish as for the Playtime Sampler (see page 93).

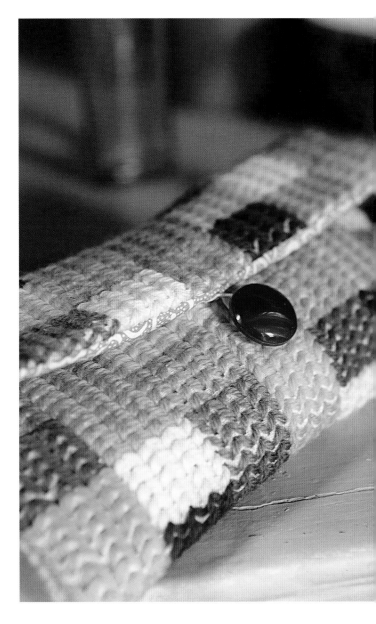

On the edge

I have always been intrigued by the division of 'work' — as stitching was known in the nineteenth century — into two very distinct categories. First there was the 'fancy' stitching or 'fancy work', which was decorative, pretty, colourful and very visible. Then there was 'plain work', the sort of thing the young Jane Eyre did at Lowood, which was the mending, darning, hemming and practical stitching, often intended to be invisible.

Young girls started with plain work and, if they were neat and sufficiently accomplished, their family, teachers or employers would allow them to graduate to fancy work, using more expensive materials to make more ambitious projects.

But every household needed someone to mend and darn clothes, to hem sheets and handkerchiefs, and the stitches used for these tasks have always been seen as less skilful and more mundane. They are practical and useful stitches, which are seen to be lower down the pecking order than their whimsical, complicated, decorative and artful cousins. In particular, stitches that finish off, secure, neaten, tidy and edge — such as hem stitch and blanket stitch — still carry connotations of dreary, mechanical sewing for little reward.

This is a huge shame, as in these days of machine-sewn clothes and household textiles, we should treasure each and every stitch when we find it in its handmade form. Even if we cannot create the tiny stitches seen on Victorian nightdresses, we still need to able to hem hand-stitched pieces relatively neatly. Even if we don't darn socks any more, mending clothes is still a valuable skill. And even if we don't have to make blankets for a whole household, we can most certainly use blanket stitch as a striking edging stitch on all sorts of textiles.

Bold blanket stitch

When I was growing up there were no such things as duvets (or 'continental quilts' as they were known when they first arrived in the UK), so I remember vividly the look and feel of thick, neat blanket stitch along the edges of scratchy, cream-coloured woollen blankets, and the way the top part of the stitch lay so cleverly along the edge, whilst the uprights were neat and firm. I used to run my fingers along the edges and around the corners, where the stitches did clever turns before carrying on along a new edge, past a woven satin label declaring with a flourish that the blanket was made by someone such as Early's of Witney. Years later I bought a huge, very colourful blanket mainly because I liked the bright pink blanket stitch that finished it off. It made me think that blanket stitch doesn't just have to match the background or be red (as in institutional or army blankets), but can be any colour and any size and any style you like. In fact, I am now inclined to think that the bolder the blanket stitch, the better.

Blanket stitch can be rough and ready, a useful, practical stitch to prevent a raw edge from fraying. It can also be bright, decorative and visible, adding colour and contrast, or it can match the background and fade from view. I like the way a single stitch can conjure up rugged, outback/Wild West cowboy blankets rolled up in little leather buckle straps, camping, army or picnic blankets, traditional Scottish and Welsh blankets and, of course, hospital blankets.

With blanket stitch, you can create a blanket from a piece of woollen fabric, edge a knitted blanket, revive an old blanket with new stitching, buy some lovely wool fabric and turn it into a bold bed cover, or use it on soft, cosy cashmere/wool fabrics to make a one-off scarf. Bold blanket stitch also finishes off an edge on a simple wool cushion.

Threads for bold blanket stitch need to be sturdy and hard-wearing if the item is going to be used a lot (for example, if it's a picnic blanket), otherwise knitting wools are fine. I tend to match the weight of thread with the weight of the piece to be stitched, so heavy blankets would have thick, chunky stitching, and cashmere would have finer stitches in lighter threads.

Decorative blanket stitch

Despite its name, blanket stitch isn't just for blankets. It makes a wonderfully versatile and decorative edging on finer linen and cotton textiles. It has a lovely utilitarian, handmade look and feel, but is beautifully regular and attractive, and there is so much you can do with it. The basic stitch can be varied with groups of stitches in twos and threes, or the stitches can be of different lengths (long and short, or long, long, short, or gradually getting longer then shorter), and it can be embellished with beads or French knots. If you add in colour, there are even more possibilities.

This type of decorative blanket stitch has plenty of applications. It looks good on the open edge of pillowcases (as I've used it here), edges of skirts and dresses (not just hems), along cuffs, collars and button-bands on shirts, on ready-made napkins and tablecloths, or on home-made linens and especially on old-fashioned sheets that fold back on beds (probably almost obsolete now).

I use stranded cotton embroidery thread on lightweight cotton and linen fabrics. I have tried cotton perlé 5 and 8 and this sort of thread does not lie completely flat, whereas three strands of embroidery cotton work extremely well. Alternatively, this sort of stitching is a nice way to try and experiment with unusual threads such as silk, linen and hand-dyed artisan threads.

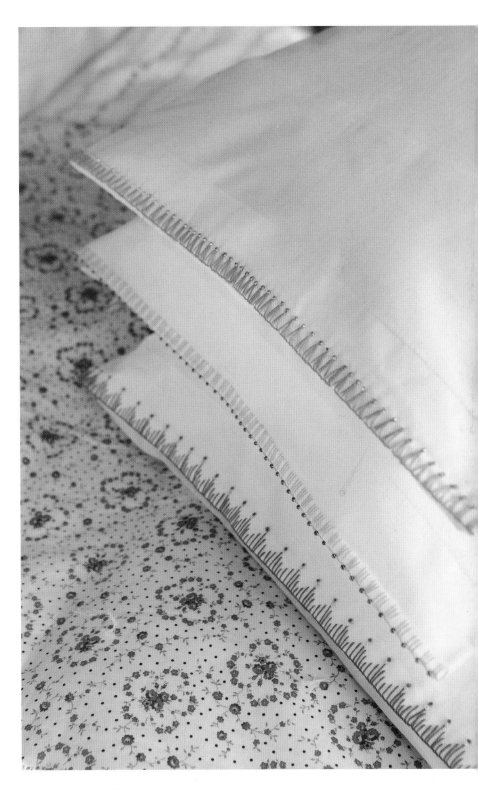

To make the Blanket

You will need

- ❖ Piece of wool fabric measuring 200 x 160cm (2¼yd x 63in)
- ❖ Tape measure
- ❖ Iron
- ❖ Pins
- ❖ Tapestry wools (see details below)
- ❖ Large-eyed embroidery needle

Tapestry wools

Blanket stitch uses a lot of wool or thread per centimetre of sewing; this blanket edging used up 1m (39in) of tapestry wool per 13cm (5in) of stitching. You will need either six 10m (11yd) skeins or seven 8m (8¾yd) skeins of tapestry wool to make the blanket shown. I used several shades of lime green, though you can, of course, use just one colour.

Making

Decide which variation of blanket stitch to use (see page 148: I've used groups of three equal-length stitches) and which combinations of colours of wools. Fold under, press and pin a double 1.5cm (⅝in) hem all around the blanket, mitring the corners by folding them as shown below. Start blanket stitching a short distance from one corner and fan the stitches neatly around the corners.

To make the Blanket-Stitched Pillowcases

You will need
- ❖ 100 per cent cotton percale housewife pillowcases
- ❖ 100 per cent cotton six–strand embroidery thread
- ❖ Embroidery needle
- ❖ Beads (optional, see details below)

Beads
If you are using beads, the hole in them needs to be large enough for the needle and thread to pass through. It's better to use the finest needle you can cope with than an overly large bead, as a big bead will look wrong on delicate stitching.

Making
Decide which variation of blanket stitch to use (see page 148 and below) and which combinations of colours of threads. Thread a sharp embroidery needle with three strands of cotton; I used colours inspired by a pretty piece of vintage embroidery (see below, right). Start stitching and see where it takes you. Embellish the stitches with French knots and/or beads.

Salmon pink with jade beads
See photograph on page 99. Groups of three fanned blanket stitches in Anchor 31. A bead is stitched to the tip of each fan with the same thread once the blanket stitching is completed.

Pale aqua with deep pink beads
Groups of three equal–length stitches in DMC 964, with a bead threaded on to the working thread between each group.

Rich bright pink with French knots
Groups of varying–length stitches in DMC 601. French knots in deep jade DMC 505 and pale pink DMC 963 are added at the tip of the longest stitch in each group once the blanket stitching is completed.

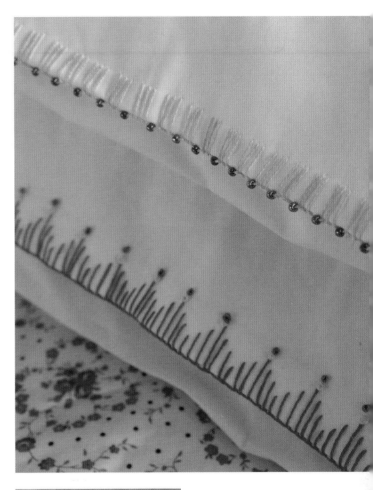

Doodle bug chain stitch

It's quite appropriate that chain stitch is one of the first stitches we are taught when we are little, as in many ways it's the stitching equivalent to learning to write. It requires the hand to guide the lines neatly through ups and downs, circles, curves and loops, and it looks wonderful in deep, inky colours on a pale background (or, staying with the classroom analogy, in pale, chalky colours on dark, blackboard backgrounds).

Chain stitch lends itself beautifully to doodling with a needle. If you think of the beautiful embroideries designed by William Morris and stitched by his wife, Jane, and his daughter, May, many of the colourful, swirling, dense effects are produced with chain stitch, which is the ideal stitch for outlining and filling. A great deal of Indian embroidery also includes richly coloured chain stitch, as it provides quick and easy coverage in the same way that felt-tip pens do on paper.

It's very easy to play with chain stitch and to create all sorts of doodling swirls and spiralling circles, patterns and motifs, and these are well suited to decorating the edges of otherwise plain items.

Hoop or no hoop?

Chain stitch can be worked in two ways. It can be worked in one movement, with the needle going first down and then up through the fabric: this is much easier to do if the fabric is not held in a hoop. Alternatively, it can be worked in two separate movements, and this suits fabric held taut in a hoop. Even though using a hoop means making two movements for every stitch, the flat, tight fabric makes it easier to control the length of each stitch and helps make the work neater. It is a matter of preference, but some projects are more straightforward when stitched without a hoop (these pillowcase edgings were worked freehand).

To make the Chain-Stitched Pillowcases

You will need

❖ 100 per cent cotton housewife pillowcases
❖ Fading fabric marker
❖ 100 per cent cotton perlé embroidery thread (see details below)
❖ Embroidery needle

Cotton perlé embroidery thread

Cotton perlé is ideal for chain stitch doodling as it doesn't split and is very easy to use. The thicker cotton perlé 5 creates nice, firm lines like felt–tips (and is what I used for these doodling pillowcases), whereas the finer cotton perlé 8 makes thinner, fountain pen 'neat writing' lines. Alternatively, use three to six strands of stranded cotton embroidery thread.

I used dark purple DMC 550, lilac DMC 553 and a lemon yellow thread that I had in my sewing box. The pink whirly curls are stitched in pink DMC 602.

Making

To draw the pattern, use the fading fabric marker, or a pen or marker that can be removed quite easily, or — in the last resort (but usually my first) — an ordinary soft pencil (this is fine if the threads are thick and dark enough to cover the pencil lines). Practise your doodles on a sheet of paper before marking them on the item to be stitched — or draw them straight on the fabric. Stitch the doodles with chain stitch and embellish them with other stitches if you want to.

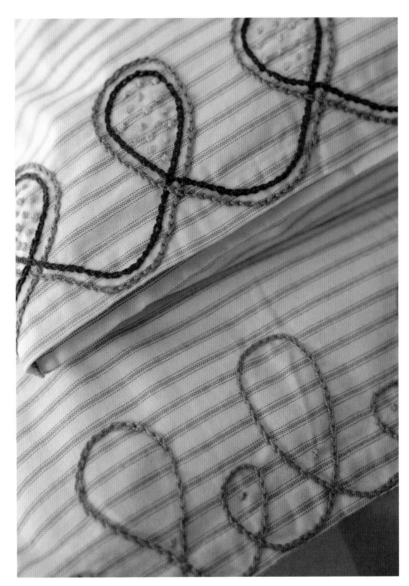

Busy daisies

It would be difficult to dislike lazy daisy stitch. It's easy to do, is open to all sorts of variations, and looks very pretty indeed. It's one of the most useful stitches to know, as it can be used to cover large areas of fabric very quickly, and can turn a plain background into a flower–strewn meadow in no time at all.

Lazy daisies don't have to be just literal daisies (although I have seen a stunning white tablecloth covered with white, yellow and green daisies). They can be scattered over a cloth like blossoms, petals or confetti at a wedding, in any combination of colours you like. I particularly like lazy daisies for their casualness, their lack of formality and stiffness. Maybe that's why they are called 'lazy', whereas in fact I like to think of them as 'busy' daisies, because they work so hard and look even better en masse, in busy clumps, posies and garlands.

Daisy inspiration

I was inspired to do some busy daisy stitching after looking closely at some vintage tablecloths. None of these are valuable as they were worked in the 1930s and 1940s by ordinary women, mostly using iron-on transfers that came with the very popular needlework and home-crafting magazines of the day. They were usually stitched on very plain pale or off-white cotton or linen, and have a wonderfully exuberant freshness, a feeling of real enjoyment of needlework and flowers, and are often worked in amazingly innovative colour schemes. I looked at the cloths more carefully than usual, examining the types of flower they depict to see how many flowers I could identify: hollyhocks are very popular, as are daffodils, tulips, climbing roses, delphiniums, lilac and hyacinths. But without doubt, the most popular 'flower' of all is very simple and consists of a central section and a number of petals worked in lazy daisy stitch, and could be any real or imaginary flower the stitcher wants it to be. The more I looked, the more variations I found, until I realised that this was the common-or-garden stitched flower par excellence.

The most wonderful thing of all is that a whole garden full of busy daisies is not difficult to stitch, and there is no real need for any sort of transfer or drawing out of the design. The only thing I found I needed to do was to make some tiny marks for placing the central French knots or cross stitches (if I was using them) to stop them becoming too crowded or too far apart. I also discovered that once I got going with the flowers, they seemed to appear from the needle as if by magic. You can just thread a needle and start stitching; as long as you can do the basic lazy daisy component stitches, you are all set to be a busy daisy stitcher.

Variations on a daisy theme

❖ Flowers can be as large or as little as you like, but if they are too large, the petals will become too loose and may catch when the item is used.

❖ There can be any number of petals, and these can be worked by going around the centre, or by placing them evenly at the compass points, then adding two or three between each point.

❖ The most popular vintage daisies are made up of a circle of petals with a cluster of French knots in the centre. I tend to mark six little dots for the French knots so that they are quite neatly positioned. Of course, the knots don't have to be in any pattern, evenly spaced, or in a circle — densely stitched knots and oval, rather than circular, centres look lovely, too.

❖ Lazy daisy petals are usually stitched in one colour, but it is possible to stitch a second colour over the tips of the petals and this creates a really lovely effect.

❖ The petals also look good with a single straight stitch in a contrasting colour inside each petal.

❖ The petals can be simple long, straight stitches or a combination of straight stitches and lazy daisy stitches in the same or different colours.

❖ Centres can be French knots in clusters or neat arrangements…
…or cross stitches
…or lots of little 'stab' stitches (tiny single straight stitches)
…or a circle or oval of satin stitch.

❖ Before you begin a project it's always best to make a couple of practice flowers, to test the needle, the fabric and the threads.

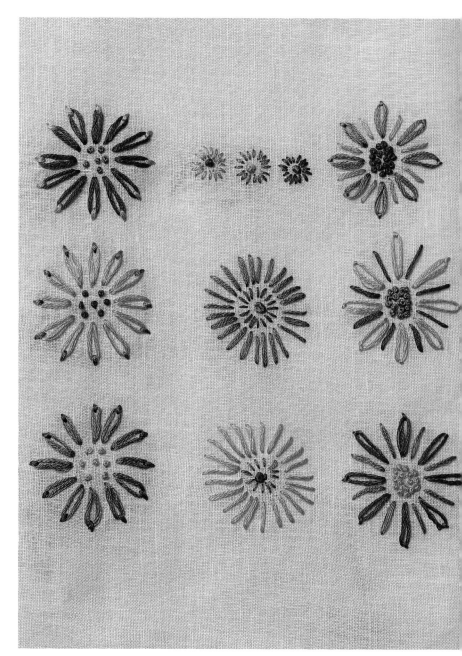

Fabric

Busy daisy flowers can be stitched on any fabric, from the finest lawn to the thickest wool, as long as you select a suitable fineness/thickness of needles and threads. However, vintage flowers — invariably made with standard six-strand cotton embroidery thread — usually appear on closely woven light to medium-weight cotton or cotton/linen mix fabric that is very durable and washable. It is good, but not fine, quality and is rarely snow-white; it's usually a rather down-to-earth off-white or ecru colour. These were meant to be long-lasting practical household textiles, not heirlooms or items to be brought out of the linen cupboard once a year for special occasions.

A fabric that is to be stitched with a relatively thick embroidery cotton needs to be heavy enough for the ends and threads on the reverse not to show through, and to support dense areas of stitching. So don't go for beautiful, very fine linen or cotton, but look instead for honest plain cotton, linen or cotton/linen mix fabric for your tablecloths. Unfortunately, due to the fact that fewer and fewer people are embroidering household linens these days, it is now very difficult to find the type of fabric that was once used all the time for this kind of embroidery. It used to come as ready-made tablecloths and other linens on to which a transfer would be ironed, or with designs for stitching already printed on. However, it is still possible to find decent-quality cottons and linens for stitching, but none have the same combination of dense warp and weft, good quality and weight, and plainness. Because of this, and the difficulty of judging a fabric on a computer screen, I would always recommend feeling a fabric you plan to embroider before buying.

Alternatively, use ready-made plain napkins, tablecloths, aprons, pillowcases and so on. These often turn out to be cheaper than buying the fabric by the metre and making them up yourself, and they have the added bonus of allowing you to get stitching quickly. Again, don't think you need to buy top-quality ready-made linen pieces, as they will be too fine for this sort of stitching; in fact, quite basic-quality table linens, sheets and pillowcases are just what you need for your free-form flowers to be stitched where they land — in corners, centres, or all over.

Thread

Six-strand Anchor or DMC embroidery cotton is the most commonly used thread for this sort of stitching, and it's what was used in virtually all vintage embroideries. They can be used in different thicknesses — two, three, four or six strands, they lie thick and flat after washing and ironing, and they create good, visible flowers. However, it's worth experimenting with different threads if you feel so inclined and have some nice threads to play with.

Depending on the size of the flower and the thickness of the fabric, I use three strands or six strands for the petals, and I generally use three strands of thread to make the central stitches.

Needles

Any sharp embroidery needle that will slip easily through the fabric without leaving holes or having to be pulled hard is fine. You will need different needles for different thicknesses of thread (see also page 10).

To stitch the Free-Fall Daisies

In many ways, I would love to find a simple transfer for a pattern made up of busy daisies, so that I could just iron it on and start stitching. But in the absence of any such transfers on the market (unless you are lucky enough to find a vintage transfer at a flea/antiques market, or on eBay or a specialist website), I've found it's actually very easy to make up a pattern as you go along. I could have sketched out a design on paper and transferred it to the fabric (see page 140), but I like the idea of an organically grown daisy garden, one in which flowers spring up next to each other in a natural, free-fall way, like the many annual flowers that self-seed prolifically.

You will need
- ❖ Fabric or ready-made napkins
- ❖ Threads (see details on page 109)
- ❖ Embroidery needle
- ❖ Fading fabric marker (optional)

Making
I practised first on a piece of fabric in a hoop, simply starting in the middle and working outwards, varying the size of the daisies and the thread colours. I didn't have a plan, although they are quite close together and ended up forming a group.

Use the photograph as a guide or create your own free-fall daisy pattern. Once you have placed the first flower, you will find it very easy to work outwards from there, making bigger and smaller flowers that are sometimes very close and sometimes further apart.

The napkins are stitched on very basic, plain, cheap but sturdy ready-made white cotton napkins (widely available); the fabric is not too fine and closely woven. I stitched without an embroidery hoop as I was working in one corner and it's a bit tricky holding a corner in a hoop.

I used six strands of stranded cotton embroidery thread for the petals (see page 144), and three strands for the central French knots (see page 149); you can use six strands if you like, but I find such thick thread tangles very easily and can make knots that are too large.

To stitch the Perfectly Positioned Daisies

Alternatively, daisies look equally good stitched in set patterns, lines, circles and swags. I used an old tablecloth with a border and central panel of little squares divided by drawn-thread work and I placed a flower in the centre of each square. However, you don't need a ready-made grid; it is very easy to mark the flower positions directly on the fabric using a suitable pen or pencil (see page 140) in any pattern you like.

You will need
❖ Fabric or ready-made tablecloth
❖ Threads (see details on page 109)
❖ Embroidery needle
❖ Fading fabric marker

Making
I stitched the flower petals (see page 144) with six strands of embroidery cotton, but used three strands for the central French knots (see page 149). I didn't use a hoop, but before stitching, I marked the positions of the flower centres on the fabric. If you are working on plain fabric and want the flowers to be in lines or a certain pattern, it is worth marking the dots for the centres of the flowers in exactly the places you want the flowers to bloom. Busy daisies look lovely on simple cotton pillowcases, tablecloths, napkins, tea towels, aprons and clothes. They also look pretty on gingham and on stripy fabrics (use the square grid design or the lines to help with placement of flowers).

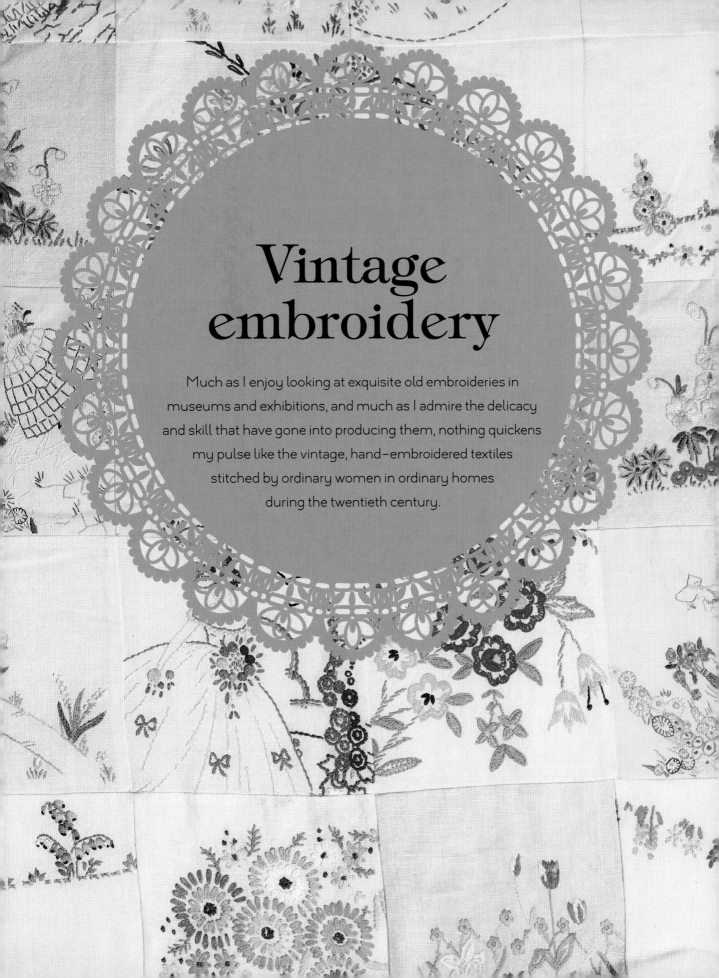

Vintage embroidery

Much as I enjoy looking at exquisite old embroideries in museums and exhibitions, and much as I admire the delicacy and skill that have gone into producing them, nothing quickens my pulse like the vintage, hand-embroidered textiles stitched by ordinary women in ordinary homes during the twentieth century.

These embroideries may not fetch much money or attract the attention of serious collectors, but they are worth valuing and keeping because they teach us about a very gentle art of stitching.

With the advent of sewing machines and the decline in home stitching and embroidery, the distinction between 'plain' (practical) work and 'fancy' (decorative) work in the nineteenth century gave way to a new method of categorising embroidery. As stitching and sewing were no longer pure necessities, embroidery became an art form. And it soon became clear to the arbiters of taste that there was a huge difference between 'art' embroidery, which was taught and practised in art schools and colleges, and domestic embroidery, which was the everyday stitching practised by millions of (mostly) women, usually following designs given in enormously popular needlework magazines, and mostly using iron-on transfers or pre-printed household textiles. It didn't take long for the homely, everyday embroidery to be considered as second-rate and second-best, and it was often haughtily dismissed in the press and in books as mediocre and tasteless.

And yet, if the proliferation of needlework magazines, books, transfers, designs and finished articles is anything to go by, there was a huge market for this type of embroidery, which suited the skills and tastes of a large number of embroiderers. And let us not forget that the domestic stitching talents that were looked down upon by the 'art' embroiderers would today be considered unusually skilled and wide-ranging. One has only to look at a hand-embroidered tablecloth from the 1930s—1950s that used a transfer design to see what is nowadays an astonishing array of neat and carefully executed stitches, including stem, satin, buttonhole, lazy daisy, chain and French knots.

These hand-embroidered domestic textiles are a vital link to our stitching heritage, and a wonderful reminder that embroidery does not have to be an art form or perfect, but a pleasurable way to create something useful and beautiful (as William Morris would say — and I would hope that he would have approved of any sort of creative stitching). They are also useful compendia of stitches and ways of using stitches, and fantastic examples of colour choice and use. Some are done in what could be described as a 'relaxed' way, but many are quite exquisitely stitched in often very appealing and sometimes quite surprising colours, with just as many deep or bright colours as pale and pastel shades.

Vintage inspiration

The vast majority of these embroideries feature floral and garden themes, and many include the well-known figure of a crinoline lady, and these are subjects that really do allow the stitcher to experiment. It is striking that the same design is often executed in many different ways; although colour and stitch suggestions were made with the transfer, it's clear that the more confident stitchers simply followed their own taste and the contents of their sewing box to create stunning, individual interpretations of a design. So it's wrong to think that transfer designs cramped anyone's style: the evidence shows that they were very much a starting point for self-expression rather than a form of mindless filling-in.

Over the last few years I have been picking up vintage hand-embroidered tablecloths here and there and making a little collection of them. I don't spend much per item and I have some specific criteria for selection (certain types of designs, decent stitching, good condition, appealing colours), and as a result I now have a cupboard full of tablecloths, tray cloths, napkins and a few tea cosy covers. After my initial discovery of such cheap vintage hand-embroidered tablecloths and the first flush of enthusiasm in buying them, my tastes have refined and I now buy more carefully, which means that I now have two categories: untouchable and touchable. The untouchables have better stitching and are in good condition, while the touchables are less expertly stitched, and/or may have tears, marks, holes and stains.

For a long time, I thought about making something with the hand-stitched textiles that weren't in perfect condition, and one day decided it had to be done and I cut into the touchable pile. In doing so, I unleashed a inner daring woman with scissors and rotary cutter, as I didn't just cut up one or two pieces, I cut up enough to make several projects. And it felt good. It felt fine to release the areas of colourful hand embroidery from squares that were marked, worn, or dull with age, and to liberate some crinoline ladies so that they could see the sunshine again instead of spending an eternity folded up in a dark cupboard.

Vintage Garden Party Quilt

I decided to use my 'touchable' cloths to make a vintage garden party quilt that would be a festival of flowers and crinoline ladies; perfect to use outside if the weather was generous, and an evocative way of bringing a cottage garden indoors when it wasn't.

Cutting the pieces

I had spent ages (years) thinking about how to use my 'touchable' tablecloths so as to revitalise the lovely stitching that went into them, and had imagined a quilt top made up of irregular squares and rectangles, cut to frame the stitching I want to feature. So to begin with, I roughly cut out as many small areas of good-quality, long-lasting stitching as possible from a number of old tablecloths, tray covers and assorted small pieces. However, the more I looked at what I had cut out, the more I wilted at the thought of dealing with a huge jigsaw of assorted pieces.

Then I saw sense, and realised that it would all be much easier if I stuck to one size of square, and cut out the best bits to fit into it. I decided a 15 x 15cm (6 x 6in) square was a good finished size, so cut out about 90 squares measuring 16 x 16cm (6½ x 6½in) and laid them out. In the end, the top is eight squares across and ten squares down (so, 80 squares in total).

Arranging the pieces

I spent quite some time arranging the squares so that there aren't whole processions of crinoline ladies along certain rows, or too many pieces from a single cloth too close together.

What I've ended up with is something like a densely stitched tablecloth, but it is so full of motifs and images and people that it reminds me of a children's illustrated book, and it will give anyone who is bored and sitting under it something to look at for ages and ages. It includes dogs, chimneys, a Welsh lady and a mountain, sprays and posies, baskets and latticework, hollyhocks and herbaceous borders, French knots, lazy daisies, buttonhole stitch, stem stitch and all sorts of daintiness and colour. There are also lots of liberated crinoline ladies in there and I have to say they do look good in their new garden surroundings, as though they are having a very enjoyable garden party.

Adding a border

I machine-pieced the squares together, then pondered the subject of a border for a few days. I knew I wanted to expand and frame the stitched squares and thought a pretty, vintage-style cotton fabric would look good. I tried every such cotton in my fabric collection, and nothing seemed to work — everything distracted the eye from the glory of the stitching. In the end, I went back to my initial idea of a very plain 10-cm (4-in) wide border, and used leftover fabric from several tablecloths (areas without any holes or marks), with a small square of stitching in each corner to give the eye a focus. I then used four of the vintage-style, small-scale cotton prints on the back as I didn't have enough of any one fabric and didn't want to buy more as this quilt is all about thrift, reusing and using up. The binding fabric is a low-key, simple, small pink dot on a white background.

Finishing the quilt

I didn't quilt this piece as there is quite enough stitching on the top already, so instead I tied it by making knots at the corner of every square with stranded embroidery thread (I used all six strands) in various pale shades of ecru, off-white and ivory, leaving the ends to show on the back of the quilt.

To make the quilt

Even if you are not as expert a stitcher as the women who stitched the original embroideries, you can use their stitching to create new textiles that celebrate their work. Once you start looking for vintage embroideries, it is quite easy to find them in charity shops, antique and flea markets, at car boot sales and, of course, online auction sites.

This method can be used to make smaller items such as a cushion cover, table runner or to create fabric for a bag. Simply use what you have got or what you can find. Choose a suitable-size template or shape for the basic piece, such as a square or rectangle that shows off the stitching nicely, and cut out accordingly. Add a border (any width) if you like, using offcuts of plain linen or a printed cotton fabric, and adjust your backing fabric accordingly.

You will need

❖ 80 squares of embroidered fabric, each measuring 16 x 16cm (6½ x 6½in) (see details on page 116)
❖ Sewing machine
❖ White sewing thread
❖ Four strips of fabric for the border, two measuring 151 x 11cm (60½ x 4½in), and two measuring 121 x 11cm (48½ x 4½in) (see details on page 116)
❖ Four corner squares of embroidered fabric, each measuring 11 x 11cm (4½ x 4½in) (see details on page 116)
❖ Piece of fabric measuring approximately 195 x 163cm (77 x 64in) for the backing (this can be a single piece or one made up of more than one fabric)
❖ A piece of wadding measuring approximately 195 x 163cm
❖ Quilter's pins
❖ Stranded cotton embroidery thread
❖ Embroidery needle
❖ 15cm (6in) of 106-cm (42-in) wide fabric for the binding
❖ Sewing needle

Finished size: 170 x 140cm (67 x 55in).

Making

Arrange the squares on the floor, or on a brushed cotton sheet that can be picked up and stored without disturbing the layout. When you are happy with the arrangement, machine-sew rows of squares into strips, taking 5mm (¼in) seam allowances (take this seam allowance throughout the project). Work from left to right, row by row, until you have one strip per row. Press the strips, pressing the seam allowances on each strip in the same direction and making sure you alternate the direction on each adjacent row.

Machine-sew the strips together to make the patchwork. Press it again, pressing the seam allowances to one side.

To make the border, start by machine-sewing the short border strips to the top and bottom edges of the patchwork. Make two border strips for the sides by machine-sewing a corner square to each end of each long strip. Press all the seams in the same direction, then machine-sew the strips to the sides. Press the border, pressing the seams away from the patchwork part of the quilt top.

Assemble the quilt by making a quilt 'sandwich'. Place the backing fabric right side down on a flat surface. Put the wadding on top, and smooth the backing and the wadding to remove any wrinkles. Put the quilt top on top, making sure it is centred and square on the backing and wadding. Smooth it again to remove any wrinkles and bumps. Pin the layers together with a pin in every square. Trim the edges so that the backing and wadding are the same size as the top.

Tie the quilt (see opposite), with a knot at every intersection.

Bind the edges of the quilt in the same way as for the Summer Kantha Quilt (see page 49).

To tie a quilt

Tying is a very simple and quick way of joining the layers of a quilt, and works well with fabrics that are quite thick (such as wool) or, as in this case, already stitched. Tying is not as durable as hand- or machine-quilting, but has been used successfully for centuries, and has the added benefit of creating interesting points of colour and texture on the top or the back of a quilt. The knots should be tied relatively close together (maximum 15cm/6in apart) or the quilt sandwich will be too loose. Knots look great as close as 5—8cm (2—3in) apart, especially if done in a contrasting colour. It is worth tying knots at points that follow the design of the quilt, such as in the corners of squares or in the very middle of squares.

Use six strands of six-strand cotton embroidery thread, which holds knots well. (I sometimes use a double thickness. I also use double thickness cotton perlé 8 for tying.) Thin ribbon and wool yarn are alternatives, although the former doesn't last well and the latter tends to felt with washing (actually the look may appeal — but if you don't want little bobbles, don't use yarn).

Choose a needle that will go easily through the quilt and thread it with as long a length of cotton as you can manage. Leaving a 7cm (2³⁄₄in) loose end on the side of the quilt that will show the knots, make a small stitch in and out at the point to be tied, pulling the thread right through. Without cutting the thread, take the needle to the next tying point and make another little stitch, so that you are making a giant running stitch followed by a tiny running stitch, and so on until you have only enough thread for a 7cm (2³⁄₄in) loose end after the last stitch. Cut the thread at the midway point between each stitch, and use the ends to tie a very firm double knot. Trim the ends to the length you like. Continue in this way until the whole quilt has been tied.

Crinoline ladies

I know that the iconic figure of stitching, the crinoline lady, may not be to everyone's taste, but you simply can't ignore her presence in the wealth of domestic hand embroideries of the 1930s. She appears wearing a vast skirt, usually with a big hat or bonnet to shade her face (and to spare stitchers the trouble of getting her features right — eyes, noses and mouths can be difficult to stitch). Some ladies may carry a basket or a parasol, others gaze wistfully while showing their better profile, or gesture to doves, pick flowers, sit on a swing or under a bower, and some are even in the company of a man, but there isn't a single one who isn't surrounded by a profusion of glorious flowers in an idyllic garden. She may be a myth, an escapist fantasy, but she's very much part of the twentieth-century embroidery tradition, and for that reason should not be mocked or ignored. Plus, she's often extremely beautiful, and her gown and flowers allow for all sorts of fabulous stitches and colours, as well as some pleasant daydreaming while stitching.

The vintage crinoline ladies on tablecloths, tray cloths, tea cosies, aprons, cushion covers and chair backs are stitched from designs that were available as transfers or were pre-printed on fabric. Some are dainty and delicate, and some are extravagantly large and imposing. And the joy of them all is that you can stitch them exactly as you please. Simple backstitch is very effective for smaller ladies (see opposite and above right) and is incredibly easy to do. Use three strands of cotton embroidery thread, and simply work your way along the lines.

I also stitched a much larger crinoline lady (see page 122) because I like her scale and because she's quite stately — not a meek little lady at all. I used six strands of embroidery thread in order to get a good, thick outline, and used whichever stitches I thought appropriate, as the recommended colours and stitches that came with the transfer (probably free with a needlework magazine) were long since lost. This was liberating and meant I could use whatever was available and to hand, and I could choose as modern or as personal a palette as I pleased.

My tall crinoline lady is stitched on closely woven, medium-weight, pure white linen, which is probably not what earlier generations would have used, as they tended to stitch crinoline ladies on cream or off-white cotton/linen mixes. However, as this lady is a one-off, I thought she deserved the best background.

She's on a large piece of fabric, as I wasn't quite sure what she was intended for. I'm very glad I didn't cut down the fabric too soon, as I saw that she would make a lovely little curtain (she could also be on a cushion or a quilt cover). As a result she now does what so many other crinoline ladies did and some still do, and brightens up any room in which she finds herself.

To stitch a Crinoline Lady

curtain, measure the fabric before starting and make sure you place the design in a suitable position. My finished curtain measures 95 x 75cm (37$\frac{1}{2}$ x 29$\frac{1}{2}$in) and is stitched on a 1m (39in) length of medium-weight linen.

The design can be enlarged or reduced to any size you like. Once you are happy with the size and fabric, tape the motif to a window (during daylight hours) and tape the fabric over it. Use masking tape and ensure that the fabric is positioned so that the lady will be in the right place. Using a fading fabric marker, trace over the motif. Take off all the tape and you are ready to start stitching.

If you are making a tall lady, I suggest six strands of DMC or Anchor (or equivalent) embroidery thread in order to get good definition. But if you choose to make a more petite lady, use three strands of thread for more suitable stitch definition.

Stitch the lady with whichever stitches you like. Look at the stitch directory on pages 142—149 for inspiration and instructions. Stem stitch, satin stitch, lazy daisy, buttonhole stitch and French knots all look good on crinoline ladies and flowers. Alternatively, just follow the lines in backstitch for a really simple but effective outline. Use a hoop to keep the work evenly stretched.

You will need

- ❖ Transfer or photocopy of crinoline lady design (see page 154)
- ❖ Background fabric (see details below)
- ❖ Fading fabric marker (optional)
- ❖ Masking tape (optional)
- ❖ Selection of stranded cotton embroidery threads
- ❖ Embroidery needle

Making

It's possible to find vintage crinoline lady transfers on eBay and on specialist stitching websites, or you can use the designs given on page 154.

Crinoline ladies can be stitched on any closely woven, medium-weight fabric such as cotton, linen or cotton/linen mix. Fine, lightweight and slippery fabrics (such as satin or viscose) are harder to work on and best avoided.

If you know where your lady is going to end up, you can cut your background fabric accordingly. If you want to make a

To make a simple curtain

When the stitching is finished, press the fabric on the wrong side. Fold over the sides, so the raw edges are no longer showing, pin in place and machine-sew. Hem the bottom edge in the same way. Fold over the top edge to make a channel wide enough for a wire, pole or piece of dowel to go through. Alternatively, hem the top edge and sew or clip rings to it that can then be threaded on to a pole.

To frame a crinoline lady

A professional picture framer will be able to mount and frame your embroidery, or you can have a go yourself. Cut a piece of card to fit in the frame. Wrap the embroidery over it, making sure the design is positioned as you want on the front of the card. Trim the fabric if need be, then tape the edges to the back of the card, gently pulling them taut so that the fabric is smooth. Don't pull too hard or your lady will be distorted.

Alternatively, you can use the hoop you stitched in as a frame. Cut the fabric about 10cm (4in) outside the hoop. Work running stitch around the circle, about 1cm (³⁄₈in) in from the edge, then pull up the stitches to gather the fabric out of sight at the back of the hoop. If you make sure that the hoop screw is at the top of the embroidery, you can attach a ribbon to it to hang the picture from.

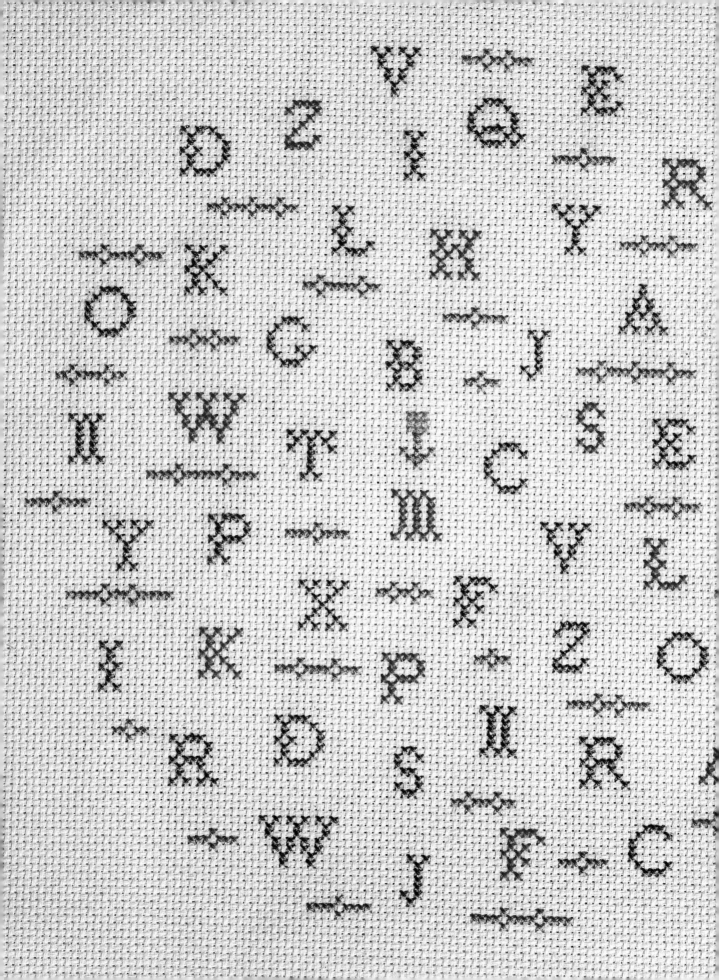

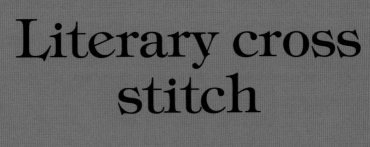

Literary cross stitch

Cross stitch has so much to offer: it can be bold and graphic or delicate and pretty, beautifully traditional or interestingly contemporary, richly colourful or tastefully muted. There are many, many charts, motifs and patterns available for you to follow, but it's easy enough to design your own pieces to reflect your tastes and interests.

Cross stitch is an age-old form of stitching, and if we look to the cross stitch of days gone by for inspiration, we can discover deeply coloured, delightful samplers stitched by young Victorian schoolgirls, traditional geometric borders and classic motifs that appear all over the world, plus timeless serif alphabets that can be played with to great effect. But if we look to places such as Japan, where stitching is still regarded as a true accomplishment, we can discover fresh, clever, inventive and very contemporary cross stitch designs and approaches.

Cross stitch revisited

Until recently, I had some unfinished business with cross stitch. A long time ago when I had to go into hospital, I needed something to occupy my hands during my convalescence. I knew I wouldn't be able to knit easily so I decided that I would use the time profitably and try something new. I have no idea why I chose cross stitch — apart from the fact that I didn't need to be sitting bolt upright to do it — but I suspect I was seduced by the rows of vegetables in a lovely design by Barbara Thompson found at a Knitting and Stitching Show.

I recently looked at the piece again, remembering why I never finished it. Despite the fact that I loved the design, I found it well-nigh impossible to match a square on a printed chart to a square on the canvas (that might have been something to do with the anaesthetic, I now realise), and couldn't believe how slowly the whole thing progressed. And yet looking at the piece again, I wonder why I thought it was so bad. My stitching is fine, the lines and spacing are correct, the carrots have feathery tops and the peas are in their pods, and I didn't make the pumpkin purple or the radishes blue in my spaced-out condition. So it would seem that cross stitch and I did have a future together, although I wasn't convinced at the time.

When I came to think about different types of stitching for this book, I knew I would have revisit cross stitch because of its huge popularity, if nothing else. So I considered the aspects of cross stitch that I do like — the beautifully proportioned letters, the exquisite samplers, the clever patterns, the traditional colours — and decided to overcome my cross stitch crossness by taking details of each and playing with them, rejecting any semblance of a pattern worked out on paper, and going freestyle instead.

Fabrics and threads

Using Aida canvas is the best way to begin cross stitch. Some expert stitchers use very fine, evenweave fabric to create phenomenal pieces that look as though they have been worked by little elves. However, it does take practice, good light, great eyesight and superhuman reserves of patience to do this sort of stitching. It's much easier to use Aida canvas, which comes in various 'counts' or holes per inch, with the holes being quite obvious because of the way the canvas is woven. The most widely available cross stitch canvas is 14-count Aida; it is easy to use, and comes in a range of colours. Buying canvas by the half-metre or metre is more economical, but it is often easier to find pre-cut rectangular pieces in hobby and haberdashery shops. This canvas is best stitched with three strands of six-strand embroidery thread.

Alternatively, you can use Osnaberg fabric or Dublin evenweave linen, both of which can be bought quite easily on the internet but are harder to find in high street shops. Both are very regular fabrics with an even number of threads per inch over the warp and the weft, although Dublin linen is finer in quality and more expensive (although if you buy it by the half-metre, you can make quite a few stitched pieces and it works out pretty cheap in the end). Although three strands of cotton embroidery thread work well, I find cotton perlé 8 makes cross stitch on evenweave fabric look wonderful.

These plain, evenweave linens don't have obvious holes, which means you have to count all your stitches and work out where the needle goes in and where it comes back up. However, once you have practised this type of cross stitch, it becomes easier and the appearance of the stitching is quite different to that done on Aida canvas, with finished results of the highest quality. These fabrics are the most wonderful fabrics for cross stitch (although good eyesight is required for them); if you want to produce a highly detailed masterpiece, this is the fabric to choose.

Needles

With cross stitch, the correct needle makes a huge difference. Cross stitch needles are fine with a long eye for ease of threading, but have a blunt point that makes it much easier to find the correct hole without piercing the canvas or threads already worked. John James is a good brand; I use size 26 for 14-count Aida and size 24 for 25-count evenweave linen.

Hoop

A hoop can make the difference between enjoying and enduring cross stitch. I don't use one for very small pieces such as the greetings cards (see page 133), which are very easy to hold in the hand, but with anything larger — and especially when copying letters from a chart — I find holding my work in a hoop makes stitching infinitely more comfortable. A hoop keeps the fabric stretched properly and makes it very easy to find the correct hole.

The size of hoop depends on the size of the piece being worked and on personal preference. I work small pieces in a 10cm (4in) or 15cm (6in) hoop, and for most other cross stitch I use a 20cm (8in) or 25cm (10in) hoop. I don't buy expensive hoops because cross stitch does not create much wear and tear, and I don't use a stand because I like to sit comfortably while stitching.

Stitching

There are various ways you can stitch crosses; you can work a whole cross at a time — forming them in a couple of different ways — or work a row of slanting stitches, then go back across that row and turn them into crosses. A simple option is shown on page 145, but you can use whichever method you find easiest.

The most important thing is that all of the top stitches of the crosses should lie in the same direction — it doesn't really matter which direction (bottom left to top right is illustrated on page 145), but if they vary your work can look quite oddly uneven.

Mounting

Although it is quite possible to use glue to mount stitched textiles, I prefer to mount fabrics on cardboard or board by stitching them into place with a double thickness of strong cotton thread (such as quilting cotton). Make a couple of small holes in the card with a sharp needle at each corner of the piece and at stages around the sides; do this by placing the card on a towel or on the carpet and pressing the needle cleanly through it. Use cotton thread in a colour that doesn't show (if you don't want it to), and make a couple of little stitches to secure the fabric, working your way around the perimeter of the fabric and finishing off securely.

Cloud of cross stitch

For my very first piece of cross stitching after the doomed vegetable garden, I did a little cloud of letters which could fall as rain and rearrange themselves into words.

I bought some ivory-coloured Aida 14-count canvas, chose a few interesting colours that would show up well on the canvas, found the alphabet I liked so much (very Victorian), and simply started stitching on fabric held in a hoop.

Well, what a difference! When I didn't have to do all the preliminaries of marking and/or stitching grids and so on, or look at a large pattern chart and then at my canvas to find the correct needle position every time I made a stitch, I found I could relax into the pleasure of seeing the letters appear as if by magic. Because the alphabet I chose is very regular, it was easy to memorise a few stitches at a time, so I didn't have all the stopping and starting and eyestrain of working with a large, complex chart, and the letters could be worked very quickly.

To get me into a positive frame of mind for this first sampler, I didn't even bother to count out spaces between letters, concentrating instead on the lovely letters and the pleasure of stitching neat little crosses. I filled the fabric with random letters (although I had to laugh when I saw, quite a while after finishing, that I had managed to put 'S', 'E' and 'X' next to each other, which proves that random isn't as random as we like to think). I then added some embellishment in the way of little underlinings (again, I varied the lengths and patterns as I went along) and eventually ended up with a very free and easy sampler that would have been unthinkable to obedient young Victorian girls, but which convinced me that own-design cross stitch is the way to go.

To make the Cloud Sampler

You will need
- ❖ 14-count canvas measuring approximately 38 x 38cm (15 x 15in) (see details on page 127)
- ❖ 28cm (11in) embroidery hoop
- ❖ Selection of six-strand cotton embroidery threads in the colours of your choice
- ❖ Cross stitch needle (see page 127)
- ❖ Alphabet and 'filler' charts (see details below and charts on page 155)

Alphabet
First choose your letter design. There are hundreds of cross stitch alphabets to choose from, from the ultra-traditional to the very modern and unusual. I am giving the very Victorian one I used here (see page 155), but it is possible to download plenty of others for free from the internet. Intersperse the letters with little 'filler' motifs (again, see page 155).

Making
Simply pick a letter and a place to start, thread your needle with three strands of embroidery thread, and get going. I began in the centre and worked outwards, taking care not to put identical letters next to each other. I tried to use the whole alphabet for practice, but think I may have missed out a letter or two. Once you have worked all 26 letters, you can start again. As for spacing, the letters can be worked close together or far apart: this is the joy of freestyle cross stitch. Vary the thread colour according to taste and effect.

Once you have stitched the letters, you can put in little filler patterns and motifs, if desired. This is particularly useful if you find there are more spaces between some letters than others, as little squiggles and lines can give a more balanced feel to the design. This sort of alphabet stitching can be done in an evening or two, which makes it a very good starter project.

Press gently on the wrong side with an iron. Trim and mount or frame your work (see page 127), or use it for the centrepiece of a cushion or bag, as a greetings card, or as a cover for a book, diary or album.

Playing with words

Once I'd done a very freestyle piece, I was ready to stitch a more formal cross stitch sampler. I'd already discovered with the 'cloud' of letters that it's possible to stitch the very same alphabet design that the Brontë sisters used when they made their beautiful neat lettering samplers (it is one of the most popular standard Victorian sampler alphabets), which means that even if you can't write like the Brontës, you can still play with the letters they used in stitching. There is something about stitching these letters that immediately makes you feel very correct — upright and neat like a good Victorian girl — because no matter how unskilled and unrelaxed you are about cross stitch, they always come out looking lovely. This particular alphabet is beautifully calculated and balanced; I find old serif lettering much better suited to cross stitch than modern sans serif alphabets.

Samplers were used in the nineteenth century to help teach young girls literacy and numeracy. But these days there is no rule to say that the letters always have to be in order. The Brontës and countless schoolgirls might have been constrained to use them 'correctly', but I decided that I didn't want to share the same constraints they did. They would have been rapped over the knuckles if they had played around with the set order of things — everyone had to know and stay in their place in those days (remember how Jane Eyre is forbidden to move from the stool as her punishment) — but nowadays it's always fun to change things around, do things differently, see things a little differently.

Of course, you can work any sort of letter sampler you like, and I decided to do a Z—A sampler to keep myself amused while stitching. It was

To make the Z—A Sampler

interesting to discover not only how hard it is to think backwards, but just how different a back-to-front alphabet looks. It makes the eye work hard and it becomes difficult to predict the next letter (although I guess there are some people who have committed the backwards alphabet to memory) and I did go forwards at one point, stitching 'M'–'L'–'M' when on automatic, and had to do some unpicking.

I made up little filler patterns to go between the lines of letters — I did keep to a set number of spaces between the lines with my samplers. These fillers are very much in the style of the Fair Isle 'peerie' patterns that are used between the more complex patterns. It's possible to create your own fillers by doodling or filling in graph paper squares, or look at peerie patterns, or use simple geometric patterns that can be found in old cross stitch books and even more easily on the internet.

When it comes to fabric and thread colours, I like pale backgrounds (ivory, ecru, off-white) and unusual deep colours. Pale colours tend not to stand out on pale canvas, and I am not a fan of rainbow-bright, candy or pastel colours in cross stitch. So I use more 'paintbox' or 'ink' colours that have a suggestion of traditional lettering and samplers, and stand out well.

You will need

❖ 14-count canvas (see size advice, below)
❖ Embroidery hoop to suit design size
❖ Selection of six-strand cotton embroidery threads in the colours of your choice
❖ Cross stitch needle (see page 127)
❖ Alphabet and 'filler' charts (see page 155)

Planning your sampler

Although I wanted to just get stitching very quickly, I did find it helped to plan the samplers on a piece of graph paper. I counted the widths (the number of stitches) in all the letters I wanted to include (the Victorian alphabet is exactly half an inch high when worked on 14-count Aida canvas as each letter is seven stitches tall), worked out how many letters per row, added up the total number of stitches and spaces in each row and worked from an imaginary central line running vertically through the piece. I worked it so that all the rows were justified (the letters began and ended in same place on each row) and varied the spaces between letters to make them fit. I also kept to a set space between each row. You may also want to consider whether you are going to mount the piece before framing and whether you might show/fray the edges: I like to leave a very generous space around the stitching to allow for maximum choice when it comes to framing. The piece of fabric I cut for this sampler was approximately 40 x 40cm (16 x 16in).

This is, basically, the beginnings of creating your own cross stitch design, something that is very easy to do with letters because they have set numbers

of stitches. Interestingly, in the best shop in London for threads and canvas, Delicate Stitches (see Resources, page 158) where I bought my supplies, I was told that more and more people are now just buying threads, needles and canvas and making up their own designs rather than buying kits.

Making

Decide where the design will be placed on the fabric and check to make sure you have it pretty much centred before you begin (any inaccuracies or slightly off-centre placing can be made good later when you trim the piece). Work out where the top left corner will be and start stitching working from your chart made on graph paper, or simply make it up as you go along.

Stitch the letters using three strands of six-strand cotton embroidery thread. When they are finished, add borders and fillers as desired to balance the letters.

Press gently on the wrong side with an iron. Trim and mount or frame your work (see page 127), or use it for the centrepiece of a cushion or bag, as a greetings card, or as a cover for a book, diary, or album.

Keep It Simple Greetings Cards

Although hand-stitched cards make a recipient feel very special, they need to be simple enough to make quickly, yet interesting enough to maintain your enthusiasm for mass production.

Cross stitch is ideal for cards as it costs very little (only a small piece of canvas and a tiny amount of thread is needed), and the scale is perfect. So I created the easiest Christmas tree design imaginable, which doesn't need any marking-out and is child's play to stitch. To add interest, I varied the colours (who says a greetings card tree has to be green?) and added a little bead at the top of each tree (more beads and decorations could be added according to taste). These cards are quick to make, and it wouldn't take long to make a good batch if you gave yourself the target of stitching three or four a day for a couple of weeks.

To make the cards

You will need

- ❖ 14-count canvas measuring approximately 11 x 10cm (4½ x 4in)
- ❖ Selection of six-strand cotton embroidery threads in the colours of your choice
- ❖ Cross stitch needle (see page 127)
- ❖ Christmas tree chart (see page 155)

Making

Stitch the tree using three strands of embroidery thread. Trim the edges, using scissors or pinking shears, or fray them if desired. Glue or stitch the canvas on to a blank greetings card or piece of flat card, using small cross stitches at the corners.

Button cards

I think button cards are one of the nicest pieces of haberdashery.
Little rows of buttons all lined up neatly and sewn on to a rectangle
of cardboard look so much more exciting than a handful of the
same buttons; the presentation raises the buttons into
miniature works of art, and as a result it's often very
difficult to break into a pristine card and spoil its
symmetry and completeness.

I can't afford to buy beautiful and rare cards of vintage buttons simply for the joy of owning them (knowing I'd find it difficult to break up the card and use the buttons for practical purposes), but I can afford to buy a few pretty or unusual buttons here or there, or a bag of mixed buttons from a craft shop. I can cut buttons off shirts and clothes, and I can look in flea markets and charity shops for old buttons, all of which means that, like many stitchers and crafters, I have lots of loose buttons in paper bags, tins, boxes and jam jars. And it has often crossed my mind that their charm and colour should be displayed or shared instead of being hidden away.

Button cards are a good way of giving special buttons (or just one lovely button) to someone who appreciates them. They look great lined up on a shelf or mantelpiece. They can be used as greetings or thank-you cards, or they can be framed and put on show so that the beauty of the button is fully exploited. Or they can simply be a way of storing buttons until you are inspired to use them — with the added bonus of being able to see them on display.

Postcards and other ideas

Instead of always using plain card backgrounds, I decided to use a selection of postcards featuring a Sixties/Technicolor style in order to make a quite different type of button card. Some of these postcards are vintage (I am very partial to pictures of over-coloured tea roses) and some are very modern, yet it's difficult to tell which is which, as it turns out that quite a few contemporary photographers are rediscovering very heightened colour photography, especially with flower subjects. The photos on my cards were taken by Hans-Peter Feldman, whose images are virtually indistinguishable from vintage 1960s flower photos.

Choosing buttons

I sorted out my buttons (always enjoyable, never a chore — no wonder children like button boxes) into groups of colours/sizes/designs I thought would work well together. Then I lined them up on cards and played with them until I was happy with the presentations and groupings. I pressed a very sharp needle through each button's holes to mark the buttons' positions on the card, then removed all the buttons carefully in the correct layout.

Sewing on buttons

As well as making changes in background colour, I also experimented with thread colour; instead of using plain sewing cotton, I sewed the buttons on with three strands of six-strand cotton embroidery thread in contrasting colours that would show up and add interest. I also used different ways of sewing on the four-hole buttons and varied the positioning of the buttons' holes (vertical, horizontal, square, diamond). Some buttons go from large to small, some have various colours, some have a colour theme, most are lined up, but some are simply in the middle of a flower.

I also made a set using plain brown kraft card for a simpler, more traditionally utilitarian look. Again, I played with arrangements, thread colour and stitching. I particularly like stitching cards in which every button except one is the same, just to keep the eye alert and looking for detail.

Other cards

Of course, any postcards or pieces of cardboard can be used. Different shapes and colours of plain card would work equally well, and writing or decorative borders can be added with pen and ink. It's also possible to stamp the cards to make them look authentic or to send a message in stamped letters.

To make Button Cards

You will need

- ❖ Postcards of choice and/or plain or kraft card postcards (available from craft shops or on eBay) and/or cardboard to make bespoke cards
- ❖ Buttons
- ❖ Large, sharp needle for making stitching holes (a sashiko needle is ideal)
- ❖ Sewing needle for stitching buttons (not too thick as you do not want it to make the holes in the card too large)
- ❖ Thread (three strands of cotton embroidery thread work well)

Making

Begin by sorting out the buttons by colour, by size, or by whatever criteria you wish to apply. Choose and/or cut out your card. Arrange the buttons on the card until you are happy with the layout.

Place the card with the loose buttons on a soft surface, such as a carpet or a folded towel, so that the needle can pierce the card easily and smoothly to make a little stitching hole. Holding the button in place, push the sharp needle through each of the holes to mark each button's position on the card.

Remove the buttons from the card, keeping the buttons in the correct arrangement. Sew the buttons to the card. Start by oversewing the first stitch several times before attaching a button. Take the thread from button to button at the back of the card and finish off securely.

Give, display, frame or make into a greetings card.

Transferring designs

One of the most vexing aspects of stitching is the issue of how best to transfer a design on to a fabric. So I am going to come clean straight away and say that I don't have the magic answer, and that as I am a believer in gentle and not headache-inducing, perfectionist stitching, I generally simplify the process of transferral, and do without the more complicated methods.

Although many of the projects in this book involve free-form stitching or stitching along set lines, there are still times when a line or an image or a design needs to be made on a fabric so that the stitcher can stitch it correctly. Here is an overview of transfer methods I use and recommend.

Pencils

An ordinary soft drawing pencil is invaluable for marking fabrics, as long as the line will be covered and the pencil mark does not show through. Few books recommend pencils because there is the possibility that a thickly drawn, dark line of lead can dirty a pale thread, or smudge on a fine fabric as it is being manipulated, and/or be difficult to remove from the finished work. But if your piece of stitching is quick and easy and you plan to cover the lines before they can smudge, then it is generally agreed that a light pencil mark is absolutely fine, will not show through, and will brush off the work. I know this to be true, as this is the technique I have used many times when I have been defeated by more sophisticated, complicated and time-consuming methods.

Fading or air-soluble pen

This is another very simple way of making marks and designs. I've tried all sorts of chalk pencils (tailor's, quilter's etc.) and find that the lines do not stay put on the fabric for very long, which means redrawing them. In addition, they often have to be rubbed or washed out, and I prefer to avoid any rubbing of hand-stitched fabric in case the rubbing-out itself creates unwanted marks. The other problem is that these pens and pencils are not good for fine detail such as close dots for French knots, or a word, because they make thick, crayon-like lines. I also avoid any type of marker pen that has to be washed out (no good if you are stitching on a non-washable fabric), which means that washable marker pens are out. So I use air-soluble pens wherever possible: they make fine, very visible lines (the violet one is very clear) that disappear within hours (though this means they are not ideal for projects that take time to complete).

Iron-on transfers

I am aware than iron-on transfers are not always viewed positively (easy way out; 'cheating') by the purists who believe in much more complex methods (see below). But not everyone has the patience or skill or even the need to transfer designs in more traditional ways, and sometimes an iron-on transfer is the best way to get started. It gives the tentative stitcher peace of mind, and gets a design that they like on to the fabric without any hassle. There are a number of companies selling all sorts of iron-on transfers, and there is a huge trade in vintage transfers on auction websites such as eBay.

The following are other transfer methods I have tried while writing this book or in earlier stitching projects.

Carbon transfer paper

This is the method I thought would be the solution to all my transfer problems. It uses dressmaker's carbon paper in various colours (red, yellow, blue — so it can be used on different colours of fabrics), which is placed on a piece of fabric. You then press on it with a pencil or special marker pen (like a biro but without ink in the ball), and a line of colour is left on the fabric. In theory.

I found several problems with it. It was almost impossible to trace a fine line — the lines are soft and wide — and very difficult to draw without leaning on the paper in some way, thus leaving areas of smudged colour from the paper on the fabric. Plus I had to press so hard to get a continuous line that my pen often went through both the design sheet and the carbon sheet and ripped both. The fabric needs to be very flat and on a hard surface, and I found that this method worked best with fine, lightweight fabrics (such as linens) but that I still got unwanted colour from the transfer paper on my fine fabrics, which would then have to be washed off. Finally, I found the lines rubbed off the fabric too quickly for my liking.

Prick and pounce

This is the ultra-traditional and 'correct' way: the method that is taught at the Royal School of Needlework. It's an excellent way of getting complicated designs onto fabric and it creates a reusable template. The basic idea is that the design is traced on to a special type of heavy tracing paper, then tiny holes are pricked along all the lines with a pricking tool. The pricked template is positioned on the fabric and dusted with pounce (powdered charcoal) using a big, soft brush like a blusher brush, then you lift off the template and there is the design mapped out in tiny dots on the fabric. It's time–consuming and requires special tools, but it's reliable, accurate, and produces fine, removable lines. If you are going to take a long time stitching the project you have to paint very carefully and delicately over the dotted lines with thinned watercolour paint, or they will brush off too quickly.

Iron-on transfer pens

Transfer pens are very sensible and practical in theory: the design is put on paper or tracing paper, then traced over either on the right side (which will produce a mirror or reversed image when ironed on) or on the underside (which produces the same image as the design when ironed on).

However, unless you have created your own design directly on paper, a design has to be transferred or traced on to a sheet of tracing paper and then drawn over with the transfer pencil. The design is then ironed on to the fabric, but in many cases the pencil marks are permanent or have to be washed out. Although this is a good method for the domestic stitcher, I still find that the very idea of all these stages puts me off stitching, and I am not keen on the need to wash newly stitched pieces to remove unwanted marks.

Stitches

These are the embroidery stitches I have used in this book. None of them are difficult to master, but do practise ones that are new to you on a scrap of fabric before embarking upon your project.

Running stitch

Even if your sewing skills and ambitions go no further than running stitch, there is a multitude of projects and effects you can make and create with this, the simplest of hand stitches: if you never learned another stitch, you would never run out of ways of using running stitch.

It's the first stitch we learn and, as such, is often underrated and overlooked as too simple, basic and boring to be of any great worth, yet the great joy of running stitch is its absolute simplicity and the glorious effects that such simplicity can achieve. (If you need convincing that running stitch can be intricate, just think of hand-stitched quilts and eiderdowns, Japanese sashiko — see page 16 — and Bengali kantha — see page 42.)

Running stitch can be long or short, with wide gaps or small spaces between stitches. It can be done in straight lines, wiggly lines, curvy lines, criss-cross patterns, swirly patterns or wavy patterns. It can be used in the same way you use a line in writing — to send messages, to create text and texture. It can be plain and practical, and hold layers of fabric together, or it can be decorative and colourful on a fabric surface. It can be fine and unobtrusive, or strong and bold. It suits all sorts of sewing threads, from the thinnest cotton to the thickest wool and the smoothest silk. It's the most basic stitch of all, yet offers limitless possibilities. It's fast, easy, adaptable, and creates lovely effects. So don't feel that 'hand-stitching' is all about clever, complex, correct stitches; you may find that running stitch offers enough to keep you gently and happily hand-stitching for a long time.

1. Starting at one end of the design line, bring the needle out and make a small stitch. Bring the needle out again a bit further along the design line and just repeat.

Backstitch

Backstitch is simply running stitch with the gaps filled in to create a more solid line (it will never appear fully solid as there is always a minute gap between stitches, unlike the gapless stem stitch — see page 145). It's one of the most basic yet useful stitches available, and I would say that even if you go no further than running stitch and backstitch, you are set for plenty of happy stitching.

Backstitch can be varied according to stitch length and if you keep the stitches neat, firm and small, it's as good a stitch as any for outlining, for delicate details (for example, veins of leaves), and for decorative work.

After a lifetime of being overlooked in favour of more sophisticated outline stitches such as stem, chain and split stitch, backstitch is now enjoying its day in the sun. Many of the contemporary embroidery transfers that are available commercially are worked in backstitch. Ignore the fact that your old needlework teacher might roll her eyes at the idea of a piece worked entirely in backstitch, because this is the stitch that is making modern stitching modern, simple, colourful, doable and enjoyable.

1. Bring the needle out one stitch length from the start of the design line, and insert it at the beginning of the line.

2. Bring the needle out a stitch length further along the line and insert it where it last came out. Repeat to complete the line of stitches.

Chain stitch

I always think of chain stitch as my basic writing stitch due to the fact that this was the stitch we all had to use when making 'pump bags' (drawstring bags to hold sports shoes) in the first year of senior school. Our bags featured our initials done in chain stitch (recalling some efforts, it would be going too far to say they were monogrammed), which was chosen because it is so neat, adaptable and easy, and makes a good writing or outline stitch (see the crinoline ladies' frocks on page 112).

It's one of the oldest and simplest stitches of all, yet can be used to great effect in free-from embroidery or in crewel work as an outline and a filler stitch. It also works brilliantly with flowers on household linens, especially if you use multiple lines and colours.

Chain stitch is most effective when worked in thickish threads in bold and/or bright colours, and its very ability to curve and coil makes it ideal for quite detailed designs. When lines of chain stitch are sewn close together with different shades of the same colour, it's possible to create a lovely effect that is often seen in traditional crewelwork or Kashmiri embroidery.

1. Bring the needle out at the start of the design line. Hold the thread down and insert the needle back through the same hole.

2. Bring the needle out a stitch length further along the design line and, keeping the thread under the needle, pull it gently to form a loop. Insert the needle back through where it last came out. Bring it out again a stitch length further along and repeat.

3. Secure the final loop in the chain with a small tying stitch, as shown.

Continental tent stitch

This is the needlepoint stitch I used for the One-Day Wonder and Bed of Roses cushions (see pages 38—39), and for the Spring Greens Pincushions (see page 40). The illustrations show how to work the stitch in both directions, but if you find it easier to work in one direction than in the other, you can turn your canvas around at the end of each row. You can also use half-cross stitch (see page 145), but this doesn't cover the canvas as well as tent stitch.

1. Working from right to left, take a diagonal stitch up and to the right across one canvas intersection, and bring the needle through in the next hole to the left of where it last emerged.

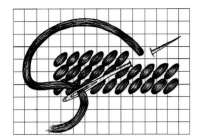

2. Working from left to right, take a diagonal stitch down and to the left across one intersection, and bring the needle through in the next hole to the right of where it last emerged.

Lazy daisy

Also known as detached chain stitch, this is undoubtedly one of the most charming and delightfully easy stitches of all. It makes pretty flower petals that look lovely with a centre of French knots, or satin or seed stitch (see pages 104—111 for a riot of lazy daisies) and it is incredibly straightforward to work.

I particularly like lazy daisy stitch because once you have worked out how to make one (and it's very simple), the stitch is open to some lovely variations. Lazy daisies can be small and sweet, large and pointy; the petals can be close together or spread out. With a little practice it's possible to make the petal lines curve out or you can pull a little more firmly to produce thinner petals. You can use a different coloured thread for the holding-down stitch at the top (which itself can be tiny or as long as you like) and it's also possible to fill the petal with a single stitch of either the same colour or a different colour. So, all in all, lazy daisy is a gift to the lazy stitcher who likes an easy but flower-filled life.

Lazy daisies can be scattered all over embroidered pieces and although they often appear on transfers, they are so straightforward you don't need to draw out a design in advance. One thing I do before starting, though, is mark out and work the centre of a flower first — with dots for French knots or a simple circle of satin or seed stitch — so that it's easy to place the petals afterwards.

1. Work single chain stitch loops (see page 143), each one held down with a tying stitch. Arrange them in a circle or as desired.

Herringbone stitch

A stitch that is very quick to do and has the bonus of looking good with very little effort on the part of the stitcher (it is ideal for half-crazy patchwork pieces — see page 74). It is also very economical thread-wise, and you don't have to re-thread your needle every few inches.

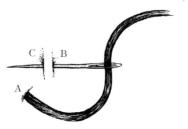

1. Bring the needle out at A, at the bottom left of the design line. Make an upwards diagonal stitch to B and bring it out at C.

2. Make a downwards diagonal stitch to D and bring the needle out at E.

3. Make an upwards diagonal stitch to F and bring it out at G. Continue to stitch in the same way.

Cross stitch

Probably the most popular embroidery stitch of all, cross stitch is easy to work, covers the fabric fairly quickly, and looks lovely; what more could you want from a simple stitch? You can use it just on its own to create traditional samplers, or combine it with other stitches. Do make each stitch the same, so that the top diagonal stitch always slopes in the same direction.

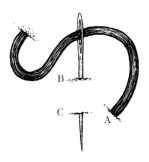

1. Bring the needle out at A, at the bottom right of the cross stitch. Make an upwards diagonal stitch to B and bring it out at C, level with A. This makes one half-cross stitch.

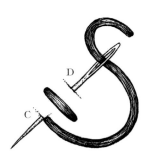

2. To complete the cross, make the second diagonal stitch to D, immediately above A and level with B. To work a second adjoining cross, bring the needle out at C again.

Stem stitch

Also known as stalk stitch, crewel stitch or outline stitch.

Stem stitch is the very best stitch for creating firm lines and the effect can be fine or thick depending on how you work it. Being able to work stem stitch is the equivalent of having a big pencil case full of different pens and pencils, which makes it an incredibly useful stitch.

Stem stitch is the grown-up version of backstitch and requires a little more concentration and accuracy in placing the stitches. However, this pays off in terms of producing a defined and smooth line that is ideal for outlining or for stitching stems of flowers (as you would expect with a name like this). Because each stitch overlaps with the previous one it creates a dense, unbroken line which is also excellent for curves (such the outside edges of flower petals). When done by really skilled hands working accurately along the line it is hard to see the individual stitches, and the result can look like a line made by a felt-tip pen. However, if the stitches are worked slightly to each side of the line, the effect looks more like a thicker twisted rope or a line drawn by a highlighter pen. A stem stitch line feels slightly raised and smooth to the touch; it also looks beautiful, so it is worth mastering and practising this stitch.

1. Bring the needle out at the left-hand end of the design line. Make at stitch along the line and bring the needle out on the line halfway along that stitch, holding the thread to the right, as shown.

2. Pull the thread through to make the first stitch. Hold the working thread to the right and make a second stitch the same length as the first one. Bring the needle out at the end of the first stitch. Continue in this way, making each stitch the same length.

Feather stitch

This takes a little concentration to get started, but is straightforward once you have built up a rhythm. It's important to find which direction of stitching works best for you: many illustrations show it worked vertically, but I find it much easier to work from right to left as my thumbs are better placed to hold down the thread while passing the needle over it.

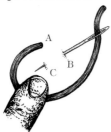

1. Bring the needle out at A and insert it at B on the same level, then bring it back out at C while holding the thread below the needle. A, B and C should be equidistant. Pull the thread through.

2. Insert the needle at D and bring it out at E, keeping the thread below the needle. The distances between C, D and E should be the same. Pull the thread through to make the second stitch.

3. Continue in this way, working from side to side alternately. At the end of a row make a tiny tying stitch over the last loop.

Satin stitch

Satin stitch is probably my favourite stitch to look at and feel. When I come across an embroidered piece that contains satin stitch, I can't resist touching it in order to appreciate the satiny smoothness, the beautiful surface sheen and the way the fabric is completely covered with perfectly parallel, closely stitched threads. Really, it's a wonder to me how any human hand can stitch so beautifully.

Working it, however, is another thing, as it's very easy to make a mess of satin stitch, especially if you are over-ambitious with scale and quantity. In order for it to look good, the outlines need to stay clear and the threads need to lie perfectly straight. It can also be very time-consuming to stitch. Having said that, I do enjoy creating small areas of satin stitch and using them as highlights — maybe small flowers or stems (satin stitch makes a wonderfully raised curved stem which looks almost real) — or the edges of large flowers. It's also very useful for monograms and initials).

The key is to imagine you are colouring in with a fine pencil that can only go from side to side, and each consecutive line must lie neatly next to the previous one without any paper/fabric showing. Although most stitch dictionaries are rather bossy and perfectionist about satin stitch, I do think that good enough is perfectly good enough; so don't be put off this wonderful stitch — just try it and see.

1. Bring the needle out on one side of the shape to be filled and take it straight across to the other side.

2. Bring the needle out right next to where it first came out, and insert it right next to where it was last inserted. Continue filling the shape in this way, placing the stitches very close together so that no background fabric shows. Keep the edges of the shape neat.

Sheaf stitch

A whimsical stitch that comes out looking like a little bundle of wheat and although it's a little fiddly (you have to be careful not to pierce the threads with the needle), it's very satisfying to tie the sheaf together as you complete each stitch.

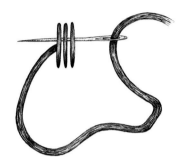

1. Embroider three (or more) equally spaced satin stitches (see opposite). Bring the needle out centrally under the middle stitch. Loop it over the satin stitches and underneath them without piercing the fabric. Gently pull the loop taut. Make a second loop and insert the needle back where it came out under the middle stitch.

Cretan stitch

This is a very traditional stitch that can be varied enormously. It can be 'open' and wide to give an attractive zigzag look, or it can be worked closely with longer stitches for a plaited appearance.

1. Bring the needle out on one edge of the design line at A and insert it further along the same edge at B. Bring it back out at C, making sure the thread is under the point of the needle.

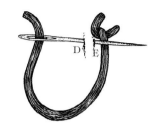

2. Pull the thread through to form a loop and insert the needle at D on the other side of the design line. Bring it out at E, with the thread under the point of the needle.

3. Continue in this way, working from side to side alternately.

Blanket stitch

Running stitch apart, blanket stitch — also known as buttonhole stitch — is most definitely one of my top three stitches (together with satin stitch and French knots). I like it for its William Morris qualities in that it is both useful and beautiful; useful for stitching raw edges of blankets and buttonholes so that they don't fray, and beautiful in that it creates a stunning effect.

The only difference between blanket stitch and buttonhole stitch — which are both worked in the same way — is that the former is used on outer edges of a textile with each stitch at a distance from its neighbour, while the latter is used around the edges of a hole within a textile, with stitches very close together to prevent the hole from fraying. In addition, the same basic stitch can be used simply as a decorative stitch in any type of embroidery or stitching (it makes beautiful hollyhock flowers).

Blanket stitch has a lovely rhythm and once you have found it, it's a doddle to sew. Although blanket/buttonhole stitch can be done so well that it looks as though it has been machine-stitched, mine never does. In some ways I like this; after all, this is hand-stitching for the pleasure of hand-stitching and not to fool the eye into thinking it's actually done by machine.

Blanket stitch can be varied enormously with different stitch spacing, grouping, direction, and length to create many decorative effects (such as a pyramid effect or short/long, or two long/two short). It's also possible to work beads into blanket stitch by threading on a single bead between stitches or sets of stitches, or to embellish it with little French knots along the way (see page 149).

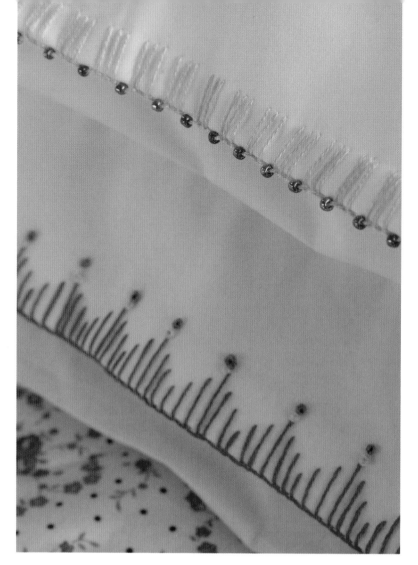

1. Bring the needle from under the edge of the fabric to the front and insert it at A. Bring it under the edge of the fabric to the front again, keeping the working thread under the needle.

2. Pull the thread through to form the stitch. Insert the needle next to the first stitch — or space it as desired — making sure the thread is under the needle. Continue working stitches in this way.

French knot

Some people love stitching French knots, and others find them fiddly and prone to tangling, but there is no getting away from the fact that French knots have a particular charm of their own, and form an indispensable part of any stitch repertoire. Admittedly, they can take a little while to get right, but once you have worked out which way works best for you — how many times you wrap the thread around the needle, where to put the wrapped needle back into the fabric, whether it's easier with or without a hoop — you will find they come off your needle easily, like little beads or drops of thread. There is great satisfaction to be had in creating a very pleasing French knot; you know you are hooked when you start grading your own knots.

French knots are ideal for the centres of flowers, but in small-scale pieces they can be the flowers themselves; think of a bed of sky-blue forget-me-nots or a scattering of little white daisies or pale pink blossoms. They can be buttons, eyes, noses, polka dot patterns on dresses; anywhere that a little dot or spot of colour with texture is needed, a French knot can be used. Clustered together, they look amazing and can be used to great effect to create vegetables such as cauliflowers.

I find working with a hoop improves my French knots (best of all would be a frame with a very taut piece of fabric), although I can make them without a hoop now. Make sure you have a very sharp needle with as small an eye as possible for the thread you are using (it has to go cleanly through the fabric) and that you don't try to make too big a knot by wrapping too many times — this might seem like a good idea until you find your knot falling apart on the surface of your work. Also, a thinner thread is easier to work with; for example, with most stitching it's tempting to use six strands to create

bigger knots, but in fact three strands make a much neater, firmer and tidier knot that won't unravel at the slightest bit of friction.

1. Bring the needle out where the knot will be, and wrap the thread once or twice around it.

2. Holding the thread firmly, twist the needle back around and insert it very close to where it came out.

3. Holding the wraps down on the front, pull the thread through and tighten the knot.

Wheat-ear stitch

A deceptively complex-looking stitch that is a combination of straight stitches and threading. This very simple fancy stitch is useful for hiding wonky seams.

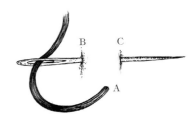

1. Bring the needle out at A. Insert it at B and bring it back out at C.

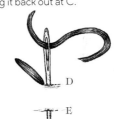

2. Insert the needle at D, next to A, and bring it out at E.

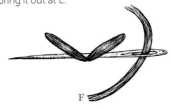

3. Without piercing the fabric, pass the needle under the two straight stitches. Insert it again at F.

4. To make a row of stitches, bring the needle out at G and insert it at H to make the first 'horn' of the next stitch. Bring it out at I to start the second 'horn'.

Templates and charts

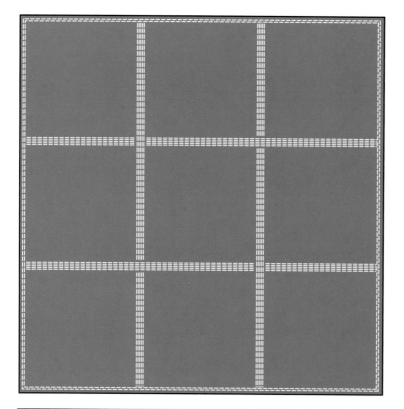

Warp and Weft Furoshiki, page 25

Pyramid Furoshiki, page 26

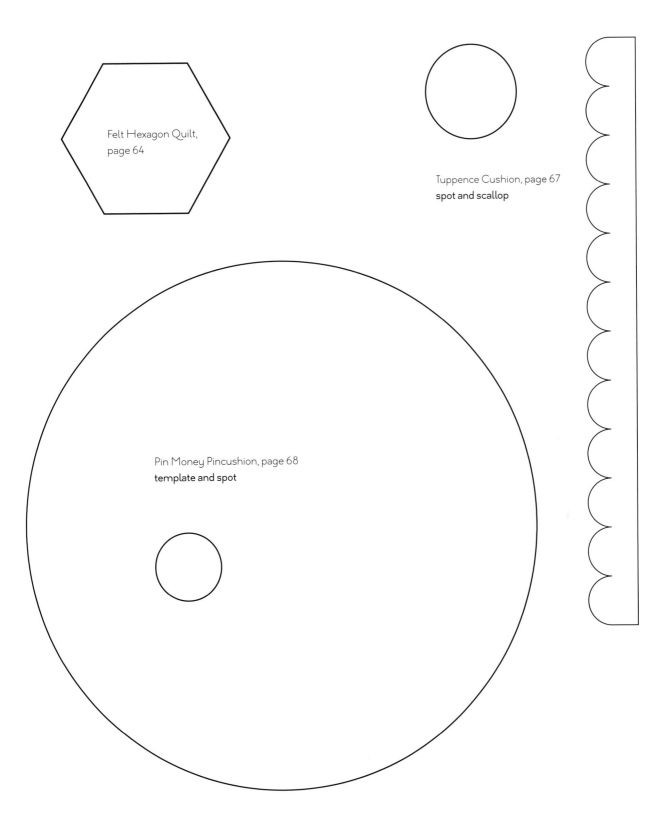

Felt Hexagon Quilt,
page 64

Tuppence Cushion, page 67
spot and scallop

Pin Money Pincushion, page 68
template and spot

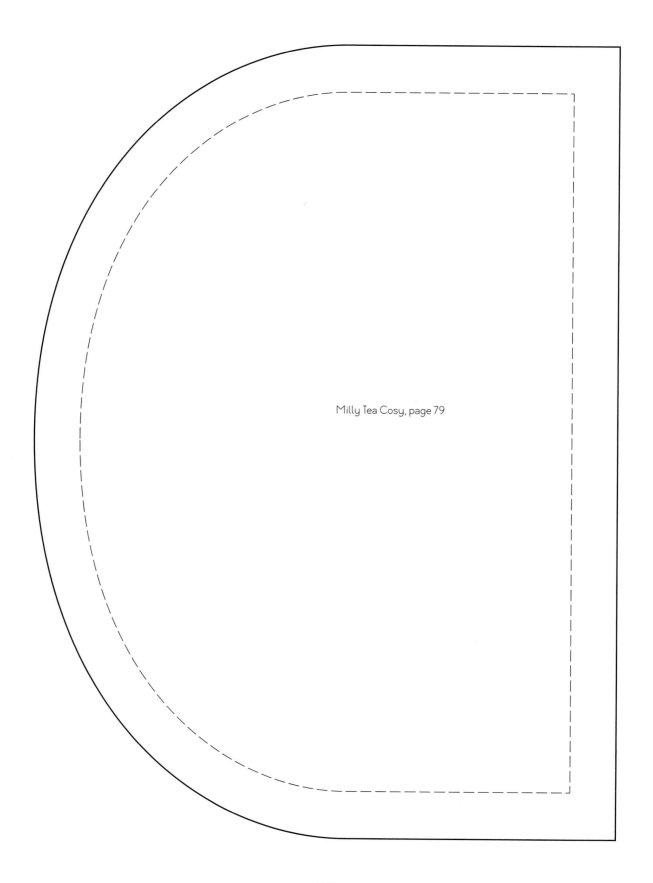

Milly Tea Cosy, page 79

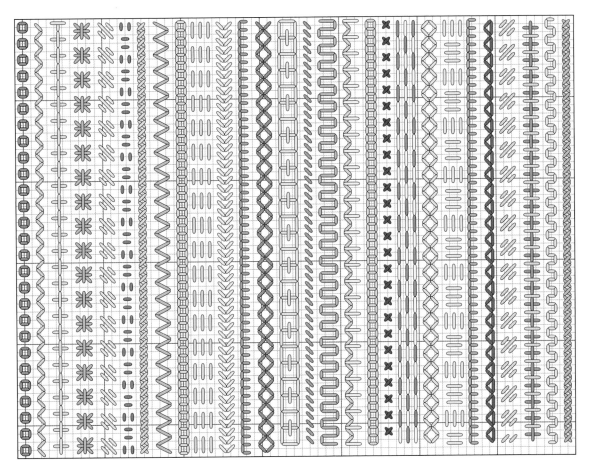

Playtime Sampler, page 93

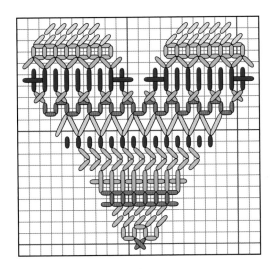

Sweetheart Sampler, page 94

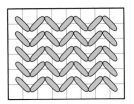

Zigzag Case, page 95

Crinoline Ladies, page 122

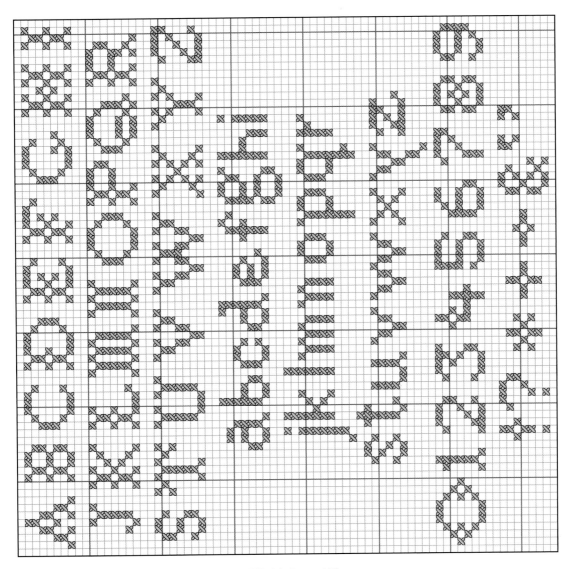

Cloud Sampler, page 129, and A—Z Sampler, page 131 **alphabet and fillers**

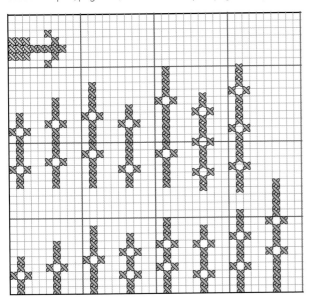

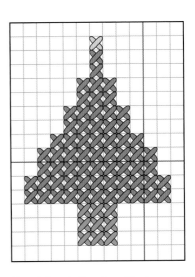

Keep It Simple Greetings Cards, page 133

Stitching inspiration

Books

Although there are a huge number of needlework, embroidery and stitching books on the market, there are very few that feature liberated, modern, relaxed, simple, colourful stitching, and most tend to concentrate on a single aspect or skill. These are the books that I use and refer to regularly.

Inspired to Stitch: 21 Textile Artists by Diana Springall (A&C Black, 2005). A wonderful overview of contemporary stitching.
Art of Embroidery by Lanto Synge (Antique Collectors' Club, 2000). With lavish illustrations and a text that is necessarily dense and packed, this is an excellent reference book as long as you don't expect a celebration of everyday domestic embroidery.
Thrift to Fantasy: Home Textiles Crafts of the 1930s—1950s by Rosemary McLeod (HarperCollins New Zealand, 2005). This is an exceptional book, filled with photos of ordinary but inspirational textiles made by women in New Zealand. The text is a series of insightful essays and the book was published to accompany a very popular exhibition.
Creative Machine Embroidery by Linda Miller (A&C Black, 2010). Although not about hand-stitching, this book is by a leading machine-embroiderer and explains clearly how to make beautiful, colourful and simply designed embroideries.
Julie Arkell: Home by Julie Arkell (Ruthin Craft Centre Gallery, 2004). Julie is well known for her quirky papier mâché creations and hand-stitched embellishments and individual pieces. This is a collection of photographs of her amazing work and workroom.
There is a fantastic wealth of inspirational material in Japanese craft books, which are so often beautifully designed and presented. They contain extremely well-designed and illustrated practical instructions, so can be used by non-Japanese readers. Buy them in specialist Japanese bookstores, at stitching fairs from specialist craft booksellers, or direct from Amazon Japan (www.amazon.co.jp, use the 'Buy in English' option), YesAsia (www.yesasia.com), and sellers on Etsy and eBay. I recommend Pomadour's Craft Cafe (http://www.etsy.com/shop/pomadour24).

Magazines

Selvedge (www.selvedge.org) is independent, published six times a year, and has an international readership. It is beautifully produced, and is the best textile magazine on the market.
Embroidery (www.embroidery.embroiderersguild.com) is published by the Embroiderers' Guild and comes out six times a year. It has undergone a transformation and is now a beautiful publication that features talented and prominent stitchers as well as news and reviews.

Practical books

Mary Thomas's Dictionary of Embroidery Stitches by Mary Thomas (first published by Hodder & Stoughton, 1934, available second-hand). A comprehensive guide to classic and traditional stitches (many with fantastic old names), with simple line drawings.
Glorious Needlepoint by Kaffe Fassett (Ebury, 1992). Still ground-breaking and full of inspiration, charts and instructions; this is where to look for ideas on colour, design, making and presenting.
Embroidery by Karen Elder, Country Living series (Quadrille, 1995). A charming and useful book for everyday textiles.
Decorative Embroidery by Mary Norden (Conran Octopus, 1997). Pretty and fresh-looking with some very appealing ideas.
Embroidery with Wool by Mary Norden (Conran Octopus, 1998). The same Mary Norden approach applied to wool threads and mostly wool fabric.
Patchwork Folk Art by Janet Bolton (Spruce, 2009). A beautifully illustrated book, full of Janet's deceptively simple, naive-style fabric pictures, with details of how to make them.
19th Century Embroidery Techniques by Gail Marsh (GMS, 2008). This is part of a series on centuries of embroidery. I use it for inspiration and reference, but it also contains many practical projects and advice.
Crazy Patchwork by Janet Haigh (Collins & Brown, 2001). My favourite book on the subject, written by an incredibly talented and experienced textile artist.
Colourful Stitchery by Kristin Nicholas (Storey Publishing, 2005). As well as many very manageable, colourful projects, Kristin offers a wealth of useful, practical advice, and her book contains some of the clearest, easy-to-follow stitch instructions I have found.
The Ultimate Sashiko Sourcebook by Susan Briscoe (David & Charles, 2005). Susan is a leading sashiko specialist and has written widely on the subject. This book has all you need to know about the history and designs, as well as techniques, materials and getting started. Susan also teaches sashiko workshops (see below).

Inspirational websites and blogs

Stitching is one of those subjects that been opened up by the internet. Until then, most stitching was put into separate categories such as 'art' embroidery, cross stitch and needlepoint, and if you were interested in more than one, you would have to buy/borrow several quite separate books and magazines. But the internet muddled all that up, and stitchers who simply like all sorts of stitching could now be found, showing their work, sharing their ideas, offering inspiration. This is just a very short list of favourite places; the joy of the internet is the linking and once you have found a good starting point, you can find yourself looking at all sorts of amazing stitching.
Flickr I use Flickr all the time to see how people are interpreting stitches and patterns and designs. It's full of groups who show photos

according to different themes and there seems to be an infinite number of photos, often with useful background information.

Anna Maria Horner (www.annamariahorner.com). Anna Maria is a whirlwind of creativity who lives in the US and is not afraid of colour and simplicity. She has a winning way with words and stitches.

The Purl Bee (www.purlbee.com). Part of the Purl website (www.purlsoho.com), the Purl Bee is an excellent resource for stitchers, embroiderers, cross stitchers and needlepoint enthusiasts. It offers free patterns, advice and tutorials for making simple, stunning, clever and whimsical projects.

Felicity Hall (www.felicityhall.co.uk). Felicity is a contemporary needlepoint designer who sells her kits on her website and has all sorts of great needlepoint ideas and inspiration on her blog (felicityhallneedlepoint.blogspot.com).

Emily Peacock (www.emilypeacock.com). Emily is another needlepoint designer who, like Felicity Hall, is modernising the craft and making it colourful, creative and contemporary. She sells her kits via her website.

Stitching courses and workshops

As I am a great believer in lifelong learning and in seeking help when I don't have a clue, I am very keen on workshops and courses. It's all very well working with what you know and trying valiantly to teach yourself, but sometimes you need to get out and find someone who can help and encourage, inspire, and expand horizons. Stitching (whether it's called embroidery or quilting or cross stitch or tapestry) is well covered in local education authority day and evening classes, and there are also many wonderful courses and workshops run by groups and individuals. These are my recommendations, based on personal experience.

Embroiderers' Guild (www.embroiderersguild.com). The Guild has 95 branches up and down the country and runs City and Guilds courses through them. Branch events are a great way to meet stitchers and to find out what is happening in your area.

Royal School of Needlework (www.royal-needlework.org.uk). The crème de la crème of embroidery lessons. Stunning location in Hampton Court Palace, highly qualified tutors and very high standards. If there is a specific stitching skill you want to learn and they offer it, this is the place to go.

West Dean (www.westdean.org.uk). A beautiful location and an inspirational environment with a huge range of courses (not just textiles). Tutors are usually practising artists, who teach in a relaxed but focused way, and encourage everyone to explore their own imagination and creativity.

The Make Lounge (www.themakelounge.com). The leading London venue for crafty classes.

Liberty (www.liberty.co.uk). Liberty of London runs 'Liberty Stitch', which features stitching, sewing and knitting classes.

Inspirational people

As with all crafts, there are certain people whose stitching work blazes a trail. Much depends on personal taste, but I have been influenced by a number of people whose work and approach appeals to me. Most teach workshops and courses, and their work can be found in galleries and shops.

Janet Bolton (www.janetbolton.com). Janet has been making her exquisite fabric pictures for years, yet every time she teaches a class or workshop her style is as quietly inspirational as ever. She is an exceptional teacher who brings out the best in every student, and has a very gentle stitching philosophy.

Linda Miller (www.lindamillerembroideries.co.uk). Linda makes wonderful machine embroideries, full of colour, texture and beautifully drawn images. She teaches workshops on a regular basis, and manages to get even the most tentative students making lovely stitched pieces.

Julie Arkell. Julie is such a sought-after tutor that her courses could be filled several times over. Her approach is to offer a simple project that can be altered to suit the personality of the maker, and to let her commentary and own work inspire. She does not have a website, and apart from West Dean and Loop in London (www.loopknitting.com), where she teaches regularly, it's a matter of searching for courses.

Marilyn Phipps. Marilyn is a super-crafty artist who lives the life creative. Although she is skilled at all sorts of arts and textiles, she mostly teaches beading courses. However, she has a very inclusive approach and would never rule stitching out of anything if it worked, and is brilliantly can-do in her approach. She teaches at West Dean.

Juju Vail (jujulovespolkadots.typepad.com). Juju is amazingly talented, writes craft books on many subjects, and has the knack of explaining how to make something to even the most unconfident student. Any of her courses is worth attending, as they are all based on the same colourful, easy-going, imaginative approach.

Lynn Setterington (www.lynnsetterington.co.uk). Lynn is an expert on kantha, made her name with beautiful, contemporary kantha quilts, and teaches kantha workshops that prove that there's more to it than running stitch.

Origin (www.originuk.org). An annual affair in London, Origin (formerly the Chelsea Crafts Fair) is one of the best opportunities to see and buy the work of many craftspeople, not just stitchers. There's a rigorous selection process and those who participate are amongst the best in Europe.

And these are the people whose workshops I would like to attend. They come very highly recommended by fellow stitchers:

Susie Cowie (www.susancowie.com). Susie made the delicately beautiful embroidered pillow featured in the film *Bright Star* (2009), and is a highly accomplished embroiderer and designer.

James Hunting (www.jameshunting.com). James has a distinctive, free style and is by all accounts a fantastic teacher.

Susan Briscoe (www.susanbriscoe.co.uk). Susan is a UK sashiko specialist and teaches sashiko workshops that are very popular.

Resources

Shops in London

The Cloth House www.clothhouse.com
47 Berwick Street, London W1F 8SJ
98 Berwick Street, London W1F 0QJ
Fabulous range of natural fabrics and unusual, limited-quantity finds. Not the cheapest shop, but certainly one of the most beautiful, tempting and inspirational. Also stocks a good range of vintage and one-off haberdashery.

Broadwick Silks ww.broadwicksilks.com
9–11 Broadwick Street, London W1F 0DB
Offers a huge number and variety of silk fabrics. A lovely place to plan a silk quilt as the staff are happy to help and bring bolts of fabric for mixing and matching.

Tikki www.tikkilondon.com
293 Sandycombe Lane, Kew TW9 3LU
Small and friendly, carefully and cleverly stocked quilting fabric shop with a great range of stitching supplies and lovely cotton perlé threads.

Liberty www.liberty.co.uk
Regent Street, London W1B 5AH
Once more worth visiting for inspiration and haberdashery. It may not have all you need, but it does have a marvellous mix of useful and beautiful stock.

John Lewis www.johnlewis.com
Ultra-reliable and usually well stocked, John Lewis carries all the good brands of things like scissors, needles, threads but the range varies from store to store.

Delicate Stitches

ww.londonbeadco.co.uk
339 Kentish Town Road, London NW5 2TJ
A one-off brilliant and serious beading and stitching shop. The range is remarkable and the shop stocks many difficult-to-find threads. This is the best place in London for cotton perlé threads.

Shops outside London

The Eternal Maker www.eternalmaker.com
41 Terminus Road, Chichester,
West Sussex PO19 8TX
Large, former bus depot filled with quilting fabrics (and buttons). Worth visiting for the range of Japanese fabrics. The owner buys with passion and it shows.

The Cotton Patch www.cottonpatch.co.uk
1283–1285 Stratford Road
Hall Green, Birmingham, B28 9AJ
An excellent all-round quilting and stitching shop and website. This is where I buy my sashiko supplies.

Websites

Willow Fabrics www.willowfabrics.com
Every type of canvas you need, including Zweigart needlepoint canvas and Dublin evenweave for cross stitch. Fantastic range and excellent service.

Sew Inspiring www.sewinspiring.co.uk
Great selection of needlepoint kits, including many contemporary designs.

Sew Essential www.sewessential.co.uk
Amazing range of haberdashery and stitching supplies. My favourite for useful, practical items that are not always easy to find on the high street.

Sew and Sew www.sewandsew.co.uk
A huge amount of products for the stitcher. A good place for blank cards, including window or aperture cards.

Mulberry Silks mulberrysilks-patriciawood.com
Silk thread in three thicknesses, and wonderful subject and theme packs.

Whaley's Bradford www.whaleys-bradford.ltd.uk
Extremely good value basic fabrics (and speciality fabrics), with great discounts on larger quantities. This is where I buy medium weight and heavy calico.

eQuilter www.equilter.com
US website with a phenomenal range of quilting cottons. Buy yardage that will fit into a pre-paid envelope to make the most of postage costs. US packages are likely to incur UK import duty costs.

Purl Soho www.purlsoho.com
Wonderful shop in New York that sells beautifully chosen fabrics, yarns, haberdashery and needlepoint kits.

Glorious Color www.gloriouscolor.com
The stockist of Kaffe Fassett/Rowan quilting fabrics. Ships internationally.

Sashiko — see page 21

UK felt stockists

The Cloth House www.clothhouse.com
Sells a range of wool-mix felt fabrics, but the colours are not as dramatic as those of more expensive 100 per cent wool felt. However, they are ideal for less visible parts of a project.

Handmade Presents

www.handmadepresents.co.uk
Stocks 1.5mm ($^1/_8$in) wool felt and organic plant-dyed 1mm ($^1/_{16}$in) felt in a range of very attractive, natural colours.

Myriad Natural Toys

www.myriadonline.co.uk
Toy and doll craft sites are a great source of good quality felt. This one sells 100 per cent wool felt in a staggering 71 colours.

US felt stockists

Weir Dolls and Crafts
www.weirdollsandcrafts.com
Offers wonderful palette of 1mm ($^1/_{16}$in) felt in 47 colours — and great service.

Purl Soho www.purlsoho.com
Purl has beautiful Wollfilz 1mm ($^1/_{16}$in) thick 100 per cent wool felt from Holland in many dazzling and tempting colours.

Acknowledgements

Thank you to everyone at Collins & Brown who helped to make this book happen. In particular, I am very grateful to Katie Cowan for her continued support and unflappability, and I want to say a huge thank you to Amy Christian who has overseen the book's development so brilliantly. Thanks also to Laura Russell for her creativity, and excellent design and styling ideas, and to Komal Patel and Margarita Lygizou for the hard work they do once a book is published.

I have been very fortunate to have Kate Haxell as my editor, and I am indebted to Kate for her attention to detail and her highly professional checking skills.

I am delighted with the look and design of the book, and for this I'd like to thank Louise Leffler.

Christina Wilson has once again been a pleasure to work with, and took the stunning photographs that grace these pages. Thank you, Christina.

As always, my agent Jane Graham Maw of Graham Maw Christie, has been brilliant throughout the writing of the book. I also want to thank my husband, Simon, for disregarding the pins and needles in the armrests of our settees as well as the threads all over the carpet while I made and wrote, and to express my eternal gratitude to him for his support and enthusiasm for what I do. And thanks to Tom, Alice and Phoebe, for taking stitching in their stride. I am also indebted to Phoebe for stitching the crinoline ladies on pages 120 and 121, and the flowers on this page.

Dedication

In memory of Alice Twist and generations of ordinary women who have brought colour and beauty into everyday life.

First published in the United Kingdom in 2012 by
Collins & Brown
10 Southcombe Street
London
W14 0RA

An imprint of Anova Books Company Ltd

Copyright © Collins & Brown 2012
Text copyright © Jane Brocket 2012

Photography by Christina Wilson

Distributed in the United States and Canada by
Sterling Publishing Co, 387 Park Avenue South, New York,
NY 10016–8810, USA

ISBN 978-1-84340-665-5

A CIP catalogue record for this book is available from the British Library.

10 9 8 7 6 5 4 3 2 1

Reproduction by Rival Colour Ltd, UK
Printed and bound by Toppan Leefung Printing Ltd, China

This book can be ordered direct from the publisher at
www.anovabooks.com

Picture credit: p30 Yuri Yakovlevich Leman, *Handicraft*, 1887 (oil on canvas) © The Art Gallery Collection/Alamy.

Index

Join our crafting community at LoveCrafts —
we look forward to meeting you!